THE HIDDEN DISCIPLINE

+   +   +   +   +

MARTIN E. MARTY

Publishing House
St. Louis   London

Acknowledgments

I thank Mr. and Mrs. Henry Becker for reading the manuscript; Cecelia Gaul for dealing with sins of syntax, and Florence Adam for graciously typing the manuscript; my father for first introducing me to these themes.

For right and permission to quote from other sources, the author gratefully acknowledges the courtesy of the publishers.

CONCORDIA PUBLISHING HOUSE, SAINT LOUIS 18, MISSOURI

CONCORDIA PUBLISHING HOUSE LTD., LONDON, W. C. 1

COPYRIGHT 1962 BY CONCORDIA PUBLISHING HOUSE

SLIGHTLY REVISED 1974

Library of Congress Catalog Card No. 62-21428

Design by Ted Smith

MANUFACTURED IN
THE UNITED STATES OF AMERICA

To the members of the

Lutheran Church of the Holy Spirit

Elk Grove Village, Illinois

CONTENTS

THE HIDDEN DISCIPLINE is a commentary on the Christian life of forgiveness in the light of Luther's Large Catechism. It is not a book of systematic theology or dogma. It is not a detailed view of personal or social ethics. It is not a historical study of a 16th-century document. It is not an exegesis of certain Biblical texts. It most certainly is not an apology for the Christian faith; it has a positive disinterest in proving the existence of God or proving the Bible to be true. It has a more modest yet clearly defined intention in the light of a particular enduring problem in the life of the church and the Christian. It asks, "What does the Christian life look like *if I believe in the forgiveness of sins?*" Because it follows classic outlines of Christian teaching, particularly in the witness of evangelical (Gospel-oriented) Protestant churches, this book may provide a useful comparison for reading while one explores the doctrines of the church either in other books or in adult classes.

Not every study of the Christian faith must be an apology directed to the world; there must be room for "second books" that are interested in growth in grace and in the church's homework. This is such a book. It grew out of the following two-phased religious situation:

Protestantism in its act of Reformation rejected the Law as the normative mode of regulating the Christian life. While certain Reformed elements assigned it a large place, all of Lutheranism and many other Protestant groups have seen the Law of God to be first and foremost a judgment on man, to annihilate his pretending self. The Law is not a ladder to heaven, a guidebook to interpret the merit badges of good Christian scouts. While legalism has been a persistent danger in the evangelical churches, it is an accidental and not an inherent danger. When they are true to themselves, they experience a recovery of the Gospel of the forgiveness of sins. Whatever words they use to express this in different ages, the reality is the same: God makes a new creation in Jesus Christ after and because the sin and the sinner have been killed.

Christ, the end of the Law! Asserting this has been phase one. However, until most recent times the evangelical churches existed either as territorial churches (the State Churches of Germany, Scandinavia) or as relatively homogeneous enclaves bound together by linguistic and cultural ties (the United States, the younger churches). The essence of modern life in this field has been the breakdown of legal support for the Christian faith. This is a corollary to the general secularization of life and the open interaction of men having competing value systems. Evangelical churches which were not inherently legalistic could be so practically because of certain social pressures: family ties, authoritarian ministries, etc. This kind of pressure is passing today, when people are mobile and interactive, when many value systems are presented as options. The temptation in such circumstances is for the Christian to say that, with full exposure and having lost reliance on law or social pressure, the Christian life will be and should be undisciplined, chaotic.

Such a view will not lack followers in the modern world. For one thing, it is in the line of least ethical resistance. It proclaims that nothing is expected of a person. Second, it seems to be consistent with the evangelical principle. For while legalism was an accidental aspect of the tradition — a throwback or a psychological necessity — relaxed and casual living can seem to be the inevitable corollary of the Good News that God accepts and forgives the unacceptable and unforgivable and sends them back into the world. Obviously this is not only a Lutheran problem. But the part that Lutheran thought has played in the ecumenical movement and the dramatic growth in size and impact of Lutheranism on American shores has brought this problem home to this church. Is it ready to share its treasure with others? Or will it be misunderstood? Does it understand itself?

W. H. Auden has spoken well for those who assign to Martin Luther much of the blame for the ethical relaxation of the churches today. He sees Luther as one who, out of the fire of his own experience, could shout a formula ("justification by faith") which met the smiling, nodding acceptance of men and women who had never trembled in their useful lives. So, too, Auden in the familiar passages of *For the Time Being*. Here he puts into the mouth of Herod as he hears of Christ's birth from the Three Kings:

> Legislation is helpless against the wild prayer of longing that rises, day in, day out, from all these households under my protection: "O God, put away justice and truth, for we cannot understand them and do not want them. Eternity would bore us dreadfully. Leave Thy heavens and come down to our earth of waterclocks and hedges. Become our uncle. Look after Baby, amuse Grandfather, escort Madam to the Opera, help Willy with his homework, introduce Muriel to a handsome naval officer. Be interesting and weak like us, and we will love you as we love ourselves."

And, with the birth of Christ:

> Justice will be replaced by Pity as the cardinal human virtue, and all fear of retribution will vanish. Every corner-boy will congratulate himself: "I'm such a sinner that God had to come down in person to save me. I must be a devil of a fellow." Every crook will argue: "I like committing crimes. God likes forgiving them. Really the world is admirably arranged." And the ambition of every young cop will be to secure a deathbed repentance. The New Aristocracy will consist exclusively of hermits, bums, and permanent invalids. The Rough Diamond, the Consumptive Whore, the bandit who is good to his mother, the epileptic girl who has a way with animals will be the heroes and heroines of the New Tragedy when the general, the states-

man, and the philosopher have become the butt of every
farce and satire.

W. H. Auden, *For the Time Being*, quoted in Rodman, Selden,
One Hundred Modern Poems. The New American Library,
1951, pp. 137, 138.

Herod — or Auden — must have been watching television or Broadway plays, or at least reading the papers.
For this weakness of Protestant Christianity on which he
puts his finger is a highly appealing feature in a religio-
secular age. The scorn of the ethical outsider has often
been reflected from within the church. The most famous
call in the past quarter century came from a German church-
man of the anti-Nazi period, Dietrich Bonhoeffer, who
began his middle-period work, *The Cost of Discipleship*
(New York: Macmillan, 1958, pp. 37–39), as follows:

> Cheap grace is the deadly enemy of our church. We are
> fighting today for costly grace. Cheap grace means grace
> sold on the market like cheapjack's wares. . . . Cheap grace
> means grace as a doctrine, a principle, a system. . . . Cheap
> grace means the justification of sin without the justification
> of the sinner. Grace alone does everything, they say, and
> so everything can remain as it was before. . . .
>
> Cheap grace is the preaching of forgiveness without re-
> quiring repentance, baptism without church discipline,
> Communion without confession, absolution without contri-
> tion. Cheap grace is grace without discipleship, grace with-
> out the Cross, grace without Jesus Christ, living and in-
> carnate.

The familiarity of that witness of Bonhoeffer's should
not blind the churches to its wisdom. Some people read
H. R. Niebuhr's famous judgment against liberal-modernist
theology and said that cheap grace was *its* forte: "A God
without wrath brought men without sin into a kingdom
without judgment through the ministrations of a Christ
without a cross." But a pause to reflect suggested to others
that it was not in the old liberal camp (which was dying
out anyhow) that the threat resided. For all its theological
fault, the liberals had at least somehow been able to produce what looked like the Christlike life. But the doc-

trinal churches, asserting the dogmas in classic fashion and going through the rituals of grace, were making a greater mockery of the Christian tradition.

For me the problem was stated most decisively years ago when Conrad Bergendoff translated Einar Billing's essay of 1909, *Our Calling* (Rock Island: Augustana, 1947). Billing, of the Church of Sweden, stated the problem in the ecclesiastical setting that I would have to face. He may have overstated the extremes, but his analysis is of use in stating the issue. Let me quote at some length:

> The very fountain of the call and of every particular duty of our calling [was] the forgiveness of sins. If every act of our task is to be derived from this source, then every such act will require a renewed sacrifice of all our own self-praise and a forgetting of ourselves in gratefulness for God's undeserved grace. According to the Lutheran teaching, the joy over the forgiveness of sins is the only joy we should seek. God will then give us much other joy, but none should be sought other than this one — certainly not the joy of selfish satisfaction, nor the joy of having done something great, nor even the joy of doing something through the power of God, nor the joy of a consciousness of growth in holiness. So we say that true growth comes when we forget to seek after growth, and not before.

> But the objection is made that it does not work that way, that it is contrary to experience. As a matter of fact, the Reformed Church has proved itself able to create many more strong, solid, and determined personalities than loose and idle Lutheranism has done. I do not believe that this assertion, or the similar one in regard to Roman Catholicism, can altogether be dismissed. Indeed, in a certain sense I think it is true. It is a consequence, in part, of the peculiar riches of the Lutheran Church. In its teaching there is but one center — the forgiveness of sins. If there be a weakening at this all-important point, there will be a slackening all along the line, whereas in the Reformed teaching many religious ideas of secondary importance would still remain to support the moral life. Naturally, this is not offered as an excuse for the sins of Lutheranism. Slackness is the hereditary sin of Lutheranism, and with the exception of Greek Catholicism, there is nothing more

slack than slack Lutheranism. But we cannot remedy this by forfeiting our greatest treasure. Instead we must seek more seriously to hold to it. Our one great discipline * must be to attain to a new assurance of the forgiveness of sins through daily repentance and faith. To doubt that this is a better way to care for the growth of the spiritual life than by employing all kinds of self-imposed discipline is in reality to doubt that God's creative power can be more effective than our human artifices.

The footnote is equally interesting:

* I have been asked if I believe that this program is practicable, so that the development of character needs no other support. My reply is, that the process is a slow one. When we notice that certain temptations make difficult the fulfillment of certain duties, we cannot be true to our calling if we seek to escape the demands these duties place upon us, but must take them as all others from the hand of God. To impose on oneself, apart from such circumstances, a system of all kinds of discipline, means to steal time away from our positive duties and reveals, too, a deep distrust of the power of God's forgiving grace. In those cases where we need to assume a certain discipline, it behooves us, because of the peril of such misunderstandings, not only to be careful not to consider such discipline, which is really a sign of our weakness, as anything meritorious, but also not to found our confidence on victory in the moral struggles instead of on the gift of forgiveness. In Lutheranism this system of self-discipline never has been and never can be carried through except rather sporadically and vaguely. It makes a rather ludicrous impression when one sometimes meets even in Lutheranism a view that all development of character really does depend on a method of training. Of this I am certain: the more we rely on the forgiveness of sins and let this training — which is not a training in the sense of other disciplines, because it has its goal within itself — be our only discipline the greater will be the true growth in our inner life. Other disciplines exist only to make themselves superfluous.

The dilemma is well stated there. Shall it be slack Lutheranism which preaches forgiveness and issues in immorality, or shall the church of the Reformation sur-

render its treasure in order to produce stronger, more ethical
lives? The problem was, of course, not a new one when
Billing wrote, though it is accented in today's exposed and
displacing society. As the years have passed since Bergendoff's translation appeared, I have been convinced that the
answers to this problem are best stated in a certain classic
of theology which should belong to the whole church but
has been neglected even in his own: Luther's Large Catechism. Out of a teaching and pastoral ministry in a young
congregation has grown my interest in celebrating the
life of hidden discipline.

In recent years there has been a tendency to discard
the familiar catechisms of the Reformation period. That
these products of 16th-century bourgeois or peasant life
need rephrasing and reemphasis is obvious. But casual
dismissal of them by the church in the name of spectacu-
larity and innovation — a sort of "confirmation-manual-of-
the-year" experiment — has been detrimental to the life
of the church. Education, particularly religious education,
should provide the learner with an organic grasp of the
universe, with a sequential, though by no means rigid
and strait-jacketing, view of life. Martin Buber calls education "the conscious and willed selection of the effective
world." If one has an eye on the complicated thicket of
reality and on the person who is learning, such "catecheti-
cal" teaching will have nothing to do with coercion, brain-
wash, or arbitrary indoctrination. Use of Luther's Large
Catechism permits one to relate himself to the theme of
the hidden discipline in accordance with ageless Christian patterns.

Even more serious than the tendency to discard the
catechisms is the parallel tendency (and an implied polemic
against it runs through this book) to desert Luther's order
of Christian instruction. As a matter of fact, the recent
past has seen a relapse into the order of medieval Catholi-
cism and a turning away from Luther's revision. The
medieval sequence was:

1. *credo* (The Creed)

2. *oratio Dominica* (The Lord's Prayer)

3. Decalog (Ten Commandments)

4. *Ave Maria* (Hail, Mary)

Number four Luther dismissed for obvious reasons. The other points he reordered thus:

1. Decalog

2. *credo*

3. *oratio Dominica* –

to which he appended Baptism-Confession and Lord's Supper-Confession to make five parts (in the Large Catechism) or six (in the Small). The argument is heard that one must begin with the creed, begin with Christ and all His benefits. Luther believed that man must first know what he should or should not do; then, when he is at a loss, he must know where to turn; third, he must have a means of seeking, finding, and enlarging on this strength. Decalog comes first in the hidden discipline. Whatever may be a good means on a mission to a non-Christian culture, our own culture has been promised so much, has been so overcomforted, overgraced, that we must begin with the demand and judgment of God in order then to participate in the joy of the Gospel.

Several brief technical points are in order. First, it would be wearying to the reader and false to the genre of this book were it to be weighted with footnotes to the Large Catechism or with proper-noun references to the Reformers. I have adopted a simple expedient: every citation from the text of the Large Catechism will be italicized; no other words in the chapters following this one will be italicized. The Large Catechism is rather brief and well organized. The readers of my book should secure a copy of the Catechism; they will find cross-reference a simple matter.

Second, I have (with permission) used the new translation of the Large Catechism by Robert H. Fischer (Philadelphia: Muhlenberg, 1959). Happily this version makes Luther easy to read.

Third, should this book find a place as a manual in pastoral instruction, this should be made clear: neither it nor the Large Catechism in its proportions does justice to the creed. I have intentionally followed the rhythms, the emphases, the spacings of Luther's book; in it he explains the brevity of the central discussion. Perhaps this could be said: my book used along with creed-oriented study sequences could help correct necessary imbalances (imposed by shortness of time) in most adult classes.

Fourth, in the interest of brevity, pace, briskness, I have minimized historical references, literary allusions, and anecdotes of the type that often appear in the interest of "enriching and enlivening" dull reading. I hope each section will hold the reader's attention on its own terms.

More than a dozen years have passed since I wrote these pages in the context of parish life. As I reread them now, after years spent in teaching in a modern secular university, it strikes me that very little needs changing. Two or three minor references have been updated. I have retained the enumerative style ("first, second, third, and the like") because now as then people tell me that this approach is helpful for those who use the book for teaching purposes. Nothing has pleased me more than the letters I have received through the years about the help this little meditation has brought as parallel reading in adult instruction classes.

This book speaks out of a Lutheran document through a Protestant situation to a problem of the whole church. It is based on the belief that the good news of the forgiveness of sins is the only joy we should seek as Christians. It assumes that, by the working of the Holy Spirit, the forgiveness of sins can be the generating center of the ethical and moral life. I know that this assumption is dangerous or at least precarious and fragile; *if I believe* . . . then I believe it can stand the test of Christian experience.

Martin E. Marty

I

"You shall have no other gods."

That is, you shall regard Me alone as your God. What does this mean, and how is it to be understood? What is it to have a god? What is God?

Answer: A god is that to which we look for all good and in which we find refuge in every time of need.

The man of faith hears this first word of Law from God and blithely exempts himself. Surely the question of belief and unbelief, of belief and disbelief, is not addressed to him. He is comfortably nestled in his cushioned pew. He is listening to a minister on closed-circuit television. Whatever else he is thinking, he is certain that the issues of that first word are not addressed to him.

He has paid well for the security of being exempt. He has signed a church roll, helped pay for a building, supported its causes and programs. He enjoys hearing the minister denounce remote puppets of state and nearby household gods. He is wearing earmuffs, even if no one can see them. Yet there is an acoustical disturbance. Somehow the word is coming through, and it begins to reach him. He is being commanded to see everything else that he trusts displaced. Only God is to remain.

In all fairness something should be said in favor of the man who is now facing disturbance. Ordinarily he faces very little of it. The religious institution to which he belongs, be its accents ever so historic and its mold ever so orthodox, may seldom confront him with the question of his belief. It has been very busy in a society of abundance, offering and receiving the fruits of affluence. Can it face the question of belief, or will its program then falter? In the minds of many people, the good name of a denomination or local church apparently suffices to give its members security. A signature on a church membership roll is often the end of the religious quest. The church advertises its beautiful liturgy, its clean, crisp doctrinal stand or lack thereof, the social position it offers. The man does his part and is exempted from this first word.

Even on a more elite level he may be excused for feeling exempt. It has become the fashion in many quarters to present the Christian faith apart from the word of Law. The note of judgment is obscured or upstaged by the offers and promises. No demand appears. First man is told what God does for him — and he need go no farther; the religious quest is complete. God never gets in His own choice of a first word edgewise. Strategically this is a poor sequence. Perhaps in a different society one may begin a mission in this fashion. In a religious society with a Christian reminiscence, something else is called for.

In Western or in American culture, people have long been exposed to the promises of Christianity. They pass churches at every corner; they are handed tracts and bombarded with signals. This quiet question remains: *What is it to have a god?* Whether, with those who pass the churches and block the signals, the man under our scrutiny decides that god is dead or whether he decides that the only thing god is, is grace, the effect is the same. Everything is grace, and the word of Law is pointless, muffled.

Suppose our man listens to the minister on TV. Now he finds that love of God and belief in Him are commanded; the purpose of this word of Law *is to require true faith and confidence of the heart.* If faith is required, the assumption is that God leaves or has left signs to make the quest of faith possible. The first sign occurs even while the sound waves still move: man is addressable. God addresses His people: it is "you" and "Me." "See to it that you let Me alone be *your God, and never seek another.*" That utterance did not not-happen; it happened, and that makes all the difference. From then on one must take a stand.

When it was spoken, that word was surrounded by other words representing other gods (just as it is now). Those other gods were perhaps the little fertility images of the ancient Near East, objects that could be fondled, carried about, adored. They would bring forth fruit from the fields, fruit from the womb. Today, too, such household gods are comfortable to have around.

Even the fascination with religiousness can serve. Or the Christian faith presented without the word of Law will do well. For this form of faith witnesses to man or to a containable God. But such faith has nothing to do with the ancient word. *To have God, you see, does not mean to lay hands upon Him or put Him into a purse, or shut Him up in a chest.*

God — unchained, unpackaged, free; God faces man in the practical decisions of daily life. Men reject God not so much because in the chambers of their academies or the chambers of their hearts they have reasoned their way past Him. What makes it easy for them to dismiss God is the way they live their practical daily life. There is where unbelief is the problem: there men act as if God did not exist.

Joining a church does not rid one of the problem. The question of basic belief is not a very live one. Not that people have lost their imagination. A cartoon shows a man reaching down into his pocket as the offering plate is held before him. He cowers as he looks up; the eye of the television camera that is kibitzing on his hour of worship is beamed directly at him, is watching him. Its external discipline will prompt a generous offering. Yes, the man cares; but he is not asked to care about God.

The person who wants to test the place of God in his life might do it this way: Did he ever let his faith interrupt a single cultural pattern? Did he ever have to ask whether military service, capital punishment, certain political attitudes were permissible if he believed? Or did membership in a religious organization free him from the necessity of thinking, because the organization took a stand? Did he ever once, in face of a schedule conflict, place discipleship ahead of his household gods? Did Christian service ever take priority over his job, his child's dancing school? How soon these questions become banal; yet the answers to them are symptomatic.

If religious organizations direct very little energy to staring unbelief in the face, listening to the divine demand, exhorting men to belief — then it is easy for man to fashion the gods he will carry around in his pocket. Merely because he lives in the Christian West and belongs to its religious institutions he need never hear the first word of God.

But when he takes seriously the question of belief in God and in God alone, he is immediately helped with many signals. Yet these may confuse him. The signals God gives are visible, tangible. God who is beyond the gods is not merely the object of man's thinking; he is present in the middle of the world. Receiving the signal, one is faced with the problem of sorting out "the world" from God. God acts. He gives man much that is good. He gives it through His creatures. *So we receive our blessings not from them, but from God through them.* What is it to have a God? It is not to have the creatures through which God acts and offers. The creatures — these idols of practical daily life — created the problem. The finesse asked of the man who works with a hidden discipline is that he sort out the signal from the signaler, the gift from the giver — and then remember which deserves his whole attention.

Here is where faith is fired and purged. *For these two belong together, faith and God. That to which your heart clings and entrusts itself is, I say, really your God.* However this faith was born when the Word was first heard, today and for us it is fashioned when man sees God not "out there" but signaling, giving, in the middle of the world. This signaling and giving he has seen in Jesus Christ, at the center of history, at the low ebbs of our existence, on the gallows, and in the freeways of the human city. When God calls man to belief, He gives reasons; without them His call is only a matter of sound waves. The reason He gives us preeminently is Himself, in the face of Jesus Christ, in the form of a rejected, dying, loving man.

This is the promise that attracts after the first word of Law was heard. *This ought to move and impel us to fix our hearts upon God with perfect confidence, since the divine Majesty comes to us with so gracious an offer, so cordial an invitation, and so rich a promise.*

II

"You shall not take the name of God in vain."

As the First Commandment has inwardly instructed the heart and taught faith, so this commandment leads us outward and directs the lips and the tongue into the right relation to God. The first things that issue and emerge from the heart are words. In the external and imposed disciplines of religion these words command us, "Watch your language!" In the internal but irrepressible concern of the Christian faith these words are summed up in the word, "Watch God's language!" There is all the difference between the two approaches.

The first, the advice that we watch our language, is well-worn. Let us suppose a man passes five hurdles in the use of language. Suppose, first, that he tells the truth under oath in court. Second, he is enough at home with etiquette to know how to salt his conversation in a socially proper way without overstepping the bounds of taste. Third, he purges his literary style so that he need not resort to a few trite and slovenly expletives. Fourth, he has a self-disciplined character so that he does not offend other people. Fifth, he does not consort with fortunetellers, does not examine horoscopes or entrails.

Suppose he passes these five hurdles. He will not necessarily have involved himself with this Second Commandment, though he may not appear to be violating it. We

5

simply do not yet know his attitude to language, the first thing that flows from the attitudes of the heart.

What we will know is that, first, he is not liable to be prosecuted for perjury. Second, Amy Vanderbilt will not consider him a boor. Third, he will get a passing grade in English. Fourth, his character will be somewhat more impressive than if he had no thought for others. Last, he shows good common sense in not consulting supernaturalists. We can even go a little farther. We can remind him that whenever in casual speech he lifts himself above the casual and says, "By God . . ." he is really saying: "Ordinarily I am a liar; ordinarily I do not expect you to believe me. Only at this moment do I want to be taken seriously as telling the truth." But so far we shall have discussed only his habits of speech, not his beliefs.

You shall not take the name of God in vain.

It is legitimate to ask, Why such concern for language? Ask children which commandment seems least difficult for them and they will answer this one is. They know all about naughty words, but vocabulary defects are capably dealt with by an adult world. And, after all, what difference does it make? Yet this is the only command which is accompanied by a threat: "God will not hold him guiltless. . . ." From the divine side, this word is taken most seriously. In part this is because the First Commandment, the all-serious one, is enhanced, enlarged, protected by other commandments, notably this second one. The religious response begins with the fear of God. Still, only acoustics, only sound waves seem to be implied in the use of the divine name. On second thought, do not sound waves tell us most about life? Human relations are formed, wars are begun and ended, on the basis of words. Words make us human; they leap the infinite chasms of loneliness in space to form bonds.

To be called to watch God's language is to address this question with new seriousness. Man, we have said, can be defined by the fact of his addressability by God.

The channels of address are cheapened, eroded, worn away, if man drags God down into his own transcience. "Let your speech always be gracious, seasoned with salt" (Col. 4:6 RSV). Keep the channels pure if human life is worthwhile, if the promises of God are valued.

The basic problem of this commandment, once society has torn down the walls of external discipline, is unbelief. Once a child no longer has his mouth washed out with soap, little need restrain him from cheapening the divine name if that name merely represents the cheap little gods of a culture religion. If a man really believes in a God whose address to him has been one of newness, he cannot be casual. The name is all. In the modern world we can picture this sense of seriousness only as we observe the energy commercial firms expend on their good name. They employ analysts and advertisers to project a certain picture of the qualities inherent in their product.

We must assume, at least for argument's sake, that there was a time when men cared for God as much as they do for toothpaste. Then, to take the name of God in vain meant to take God in vain, to cheapen and pull Him down. Jesus spoke of His work as manifesting His Father's name. If one obscures this name, the whole saving plan of God is removed from reach.

When the man of faith hears this command, he is not beginning at the beginning. He does not hear a naked, cold word, coming "out of the blue," as it were. He is in a covenanted community of people, recognized as the created, the redeemed. A hell-torn, heaven-storming being, he would care about the use of the name that has changed him. If he cares, he will not bring that name into guilt by association, to advance his own causes.

To discuss it briefly, misuse of the divine name occurs most obviously in worldly business and in matters involving money, property, and honor. If men claim to believe in God, a business ethic can begin to be developed out of this command. Misuse of the name *is especially common in marriage matters.* If both parties profess to believe, marital counseling will have to be orbited into range of this command. The other has staked his or her future on a word given in the presence of God; that word and thus that God are dragged down when the bond is broken. *The greatest abuse, however, occurs in spiritual matters, which pertain to the conscience, when false preachers arise and peddle their lying nonsense as the Word of God.*

See, all this is an attempt to embellish yourself with God's name. . . . It is man versus God. Man does well not to waste the name of God, making it useless for profound religious discourse. Bad etiquette and a meager vocabulary play their part. But tossing the name of God meaninglessly around the marketplace of religiousness renders it useless to point to the God who spoke this word.

Watch God's language, because it is the language of love designed to help man. "Call upon Me in the day of trouble," invites God. "At the name of Jesus every knee should bow," said an ancient Christian hymn. Jesus kept His Father's name intact, unimpaired, treasured; it signified the divine presence. He spoke a new language of love. At a place called the Place of a Skull He died to keep the name's holiness inviolate, its love spreading. The community of those who witnessed His resurrection called themselves the adopted. They belonged; they, too, were sons. It has always seemed good for some to watch over the use of the family name. If they believed in it.

"You shall sanctify the holy day."

This word was not spoken as part of a church-attendance crusade or to build up a religious institution. It meant something for the good of man and for belief in God. The external discipline compelling formal obedience to it was removed long ago: *as far as outward observance is con-*

cerned, the commandment was given to the Jews alone.
The more nearly modern impositions of the commandment
have also been forgotten. A child once was conscious that
he was in church not so much because of the all-seeing
eye of God as because of the all-seeing eye of Aunt Martha,
looking down from the balcony. People who are free,
mature, mobile, who go from place to place, are less conscious of oppressive disciplines forcing them to keep a day
holy. All is thrown on an inner discipline of loving response ↵
to a word and a situation.

This third word is really addressed to the question, Who
owns time? The Law of God has much to say in the way
of threat concerning misuse of time and of promise concerning redemption of time. Basically, three questions are
implied here, as to time and work, time and rest, time and
worship. Only two are dealt with explicitly. Curiously,
the issue of rest comes first; we are naturally quite happy
about that until we listen!

We keep [holy days] first for the sake of bodily need.
Nature teaches and demands that the common people . . .
should retire for a day to rest and be refreshed. You shall
hallow this day of rest. That there shall be a day of rest
is pretty well established in a society which may soon
decree three such days each week. Who owns rest time?
Since we observe holidays anyhow, we should devote their
observance to learning *God's Word.* Here God's Word is
attached to the rhythms of the week; a religious observance
hitchhikes on a bodily need. Again it is legitimate to ask
whether this command needs to be commanded. When we
probe deeper, all this is thrown into a different light.
We usually see rest compulsively, as a desperate attempt to
fill a vacuum that the absence of meaning and work leaves.
Actually we would understand this matter better if we
could see it in reverse: rest as a cure for the work-sickness
of our times. God rested, according to ancient belief, not
because He was tired but to crown the week. Man stays
away from work one day especially to hallow that day. But
in our times it does not often turn out like that. The day

of rest is usually the busiest for lifeguards, policemen, vice squads, and ambulances. The ways we break the boredom of our life show how desperate that boredom is.

If God owns man's rest time, and man really believes in God, then man is asked to rest in God, as part of God's plan. What are you when you are not in the middle of furious action? That is the way to put the question. Are you hollow, vain, restless, uncreative? Great art, including the great art of living, is forged on the day of rest.

Who owns time? The parallel question concerns the belief in, the name of, and the Word of God. God's Word shapes the world, shapes the day. The day is therefore holy. Each man must ask whether it is holy for him. The day of the resurrection, observed by the church of the hidden discipline, is a day of newness. New people come out of the grave of Baptism. New men and women walk away from the table of the anticipated heavenly banquet. New men and women are formed by the divine Word. *Secondly and most especially, we keep holy days so that people may have time and opportunity, which otherwise would not be available, to participate in public worship, that is, that they may assemble to hear and discuss God's Word and then praise God with song and prayer.*

There is no law about observing the day.

But if on the day the Word of God breaks the acoustical barrier and the sacrament of sound waves re-creates the assembly of believers, then everything is thrown into a new dimension. Who owns time? He who shapes the day with His Word. There is no room here for all the nonsense about worshiping God on the Lord's day, the day of resurrection, with an ear on Beethoven and a hand on a highball; with a golf club or fishing reel and an ear on a transistor radio. It is the Word of God which saves, and he who cuts himself off from that Word publishes his unbelief and cuts himself off from its saving power. The hidden flock gathers. The one who absents himself does not merely complicate the statistics of a church-attendance crusade (hardly any question could be less important);

he repudiates the discipline of the gathered. He asserts
not his low imagination but his unbelief; and he asserts it
by a low-effort devotion to the Word on its day.

*Therefore this commandment is violated not only by
those who grossly misuse and desecrate the holy day, like
those who in their greed or frivolity neglect to hear God's
Word or lie around in taverns dead drunk like swine, but
also by that multitude of others who listen to God's Word
as they would to any other entertainment. . . .* The sequence
is seen to be something like this:

1. Ordinarily man works, because God owns time.

2. Because God owns time, man follows Him and crowns
the week with rest.

3. Since man is resting anyhow, he does well to hear the
Word of God.

4. That Word will make new demands on him to re-
create him.

The man who absents himself from attention to this
Word is declaring the real absence of Christ in the Lord's
Supper, is asserting that Baptism is a nice trivial rite.
He sees the Word to be a stereophonic study in illusion.
To see so much in the day of rest is difficult. It implies
that in the liturgy something decisive really happens.
It does not not-happen. God is present.

Man has to work at this to learn this language of rest
and recreation. To say that this language comes naturally
is folly. A great Christian used to say, "I kiss my child not
only because I love her, but in order to love her." So it is
with worship and its disciplines. Hearing the Word in the
gathering is the social celebration of the love of God.

IV

"You shall honor your father and mother."

The words move from the vertical dimension — concern
for belief, for the name, for the Lord — to the horizontal.

11

The first and greatest of the commands for man among men is this word against anarchy. Here most of all the hidden discipline of the forgiven life will be called into activity. Here most of all the old, externally imposed disciplines of laws and social pressures break down in the modern world. Here man has to want to see order, authority, family life, in the light of the Word of God.

The command raises many issues, and it will be well to concentrate only on one cluster. This centers in the idea that it *is a much greater thing to honor than to love. Honor includes not only love, but also deference, humility, and modesty, directed (so to speak) toward a majesty hidden within them* (parents, superiors, etc.). A "hidden majesty." The mind's eye immediately pictures the radical character of that hiddenness. An inebriated father, a shrewish mother, a neglectful parental pattern — these hardly signal innate majesty. That is precisely true: the first concern of the fourth word is to throw the question away from arbitrary personality matters and to ground human relations on the judging and providing Word of God.

Since the commands of God force everyone to consider questions of belief in God and regard for the neighbor, the first temptation will always be to exempt oneself from their concerns. In this instance, exemption is easy. Offhand I can think of five dodges. First, I may have no parents; I have outlived the years of this command, and God removes its sting for me by the mere outpacing chronology of my life. Second, say that I do honor my parents. I fall all over them with honor. I do not even have to develop my own personality, my own integrity, so sure am I of the honor with which I surround them. Third, suppose my standards — divinely oriented — conflict with and outdistance my parents? Shall I make cheap compromises because of a nonexistent *"hidden majesty"*? Adults in a fluid, mobile society can find an even better dodge: my parents are at a safe distance. It is not difficult to honor them so long as I see them only a few days a year. Finally, and with greatest legitimacy, I may say that things have changed and that the command now is to be seen in a new light.

This last has much warrant in fact. Our complex, technical society has many built-in safeguards for order which the wandering tribes of the ancient Near East did not have. They necessarily organized around clan, family, parent. And the agrarian society, the peasant world of the 16th century, held entirely different presuppositions about man and his parent, man and authority. Again, this is correct and must be noisily asserted, in order for us to get at the real meaning of the command.

We are helped by the fact that the Fourth Commandment has but one concern. Today's world can relieve it of the task of carrying unnecessary baggage. The command is not a book on infant and child care, a sociological study of the dynamics of parent-child relations. It is not a medical manual, a psychiatric treatise, a book of advice on how to do it. When the believer distorts it for these purposes, its original task is lost. That original task is the throwing of the whole weight of human society on the power of the Word of God. Out of that Word and after it the medical manuals and the practical treatises have a legitimate place.

The first thing the Word of God can do for the family is to rescue it from its dependent status. Even though we may often appear to be worshiping the family, we do so because we are doubtful over its status. First we hook on to as many aspects of our technical society as possible, and then we fit the family or the church in. Family tradition, family concern, family dinner, family observances — these are worshiped and idolized in symbol as they pass into obscurity. We turn to sociology, psychology, and the advice columns in the newspapers for pictures of family solutions. "My doctor says . . ." has become the absolute oracle to displace "Thus says the Lord." (This is as embarrassing to doctors as it is unfair to their discipline.) In the frantic and furious quest for family security in a buffeting society, we must sooner or later come back to reexplore the place the Word of God might play.

The Christian tradition sees in this command a parental symbol for authority on which all order is based. Basically this is the command which wars against anarchy, against the breakdown of order, the disintegration of God's mandates. The parent then implies that God has representatives in the world of man; that they are visible persons; that the Word of God gives their position a hidden majesty. Only then come all the questions about the competence, the distance, the place of parents. What has not changed from the days of tribalism and peasantdom is the fact that the Word of God, as old as Genesis, sets up the orders of men's relations to one another. They are not simply contracts or agreements; they are grounded in the eternal order of things, an order made visible and present when the Word is spoken.

God is invisible. Man is visible. Parents are representatives of the claim of the invisible in the world of daily life. They are not free to carry out their work if they are not accorded honor, which includes love, deference, humility — this much is established. Young people may find parents to be *lowly, poor, feeble, and eccentric* (see, modern problems were anticipated!). *We are not to think of their persons . . . but of the will of God.* This dictum puts the quest into a different dimension. Chesterton may have been right: he said he could picture happy families, but not compatible ones. Families built only on the quest for cozily related personalities will hardly be able to sustain the weight of the conflict of generations.

What does such a conception do for children? Jesus, in setting forth the child as being a first example in the Kingdom, knew what He was doing theologically (in the plan of God) and psychologically (in the mind of the child). The dependent aspect of belief and the imagination associated with belief in God are more dramatic in the life of a child than in an adult. A child unimpressed by what the child-care manuals say is more impressed by what his belief involves. Try the experiment with a group of children: ask them which command of God is the most difficult for them to keep; they will ordinarily cite this one. Out of these stirrings of conscience the creative response can come — provided the parent, whose imagination is often less vivid and whose belief is often dulled, can then be shown the disciplines of parental life.

This command does not permit the parent to be arbitrary or authoritarian. The Word of God establishes the parent-child relation as one of security, because it resides *in the will of God,* and at the same time reminds us of the parents' personhood. *If we had no father and mother, we should wish, on account of the commandment, that God would set up a block or a stone which we might call father and mother. How much more, when He has given us living parents, should we be happy to show them honor and obedience!* The hidden discipline lives off intensity of faith and of concern for the other person: now the parent is seen as a sinner, as one forgiven or potentially forgiven.

Violation of this personal element may come from either side. When the child regards the parent as a commanding robot, he has made the parent into a thing. The parent, too, must see the child as a person. *Everybody acts as if God gave us children for our pleasure and amusement.* No, the child exists for his own sake and for God's. This fact removes romantic conceptions of parent-child, child-teacher, employer-employee, ruler-citizen relations. Marriage exists not to produce children but to produce children of God. The state exists first for the city of man, but it must give its residents freedom for the pilgrimage to the city of God.

"Will of God," "Word of God" — these can be rather cold terms for warm realities. The Biblical picture is more rich. Here are several of its facets: First, the pattern of honor implied by the word here involves a change in the understanding of the basis of relations. The heavenly Father is not just a projection of the human picture of the earthly father, not just a need-fulfiller. Rather, the earthly father has his prototype in the heavenly Father. In the story of the Prodigal Son we do not have "an earthly story with a heavenly meaning" (a popular definition of a parable) but "a heavenly story with an earthly setting." The point is not: "This is how fathers are, so this is how God is"; rather it is: "This is how God is. Here is a pattern for fatherhood."

Second, the relation of the Father to Jesus Christ is a pattern for all sonship. Here is a perfect picture of obedience apart from the Law because of a conformity of wills. So with the Fourth Commandment: if parent and child each seek the will of God, they grow more and more into a relation which needs less emphasis on Law. Third, Jesus Christ by His life and death restores wholeness after the brokenness that always comes into the life of the family, the school, the church, the civil society. He stands between the related parties, by His life reaffirming this word of God. Fourth, the family and the other institutions of God exist as workshops for character, where Christ's virtues are lived out. Fifth, where the will of God is operative in human affairs, there is freedom.

There is no freedom in anarchy or in authoritarianism. The anarchist and his victim are not free. The authoritarian personality and his victim are not free. Only where Christian newness comes into play in the light of the command is there freedom. Hitler's transplanted families, Russia's controlled families, Red China's ant-heap communes — and America's eroding family structure — are threats to freedom because they violate God's mandates and orders. Unbelief and unconcern for the other have their way.

If this command is placed on the parent and he hears and believes it, he stands the chance of growing into what it expects him to be; if it is placed on the child and he hears and believes it, he also can conform more readily to the likeness it sets forth. Otherwise — if it is given a base only in psychology, in emotion — the center of the family cannot hold.

An epitaph of the past described a parent: "She touched the soil of Virginia with her little foot, and the wilderness became a home." One need not ask questions about her belief or her concern for others. The fruit describes the seed; the result presupposes the causes. "She" would not be pictured as ruling in an authoritarian manner. The portrait of her, drawn in the time of the modern world's dawning, applies to any time, any place where human relations are built on the relations to God. That pattern seems to be just about our last chance, before anarchy or authoritarianism takes over and has its day — a last day.

V

"You shall not kill."

To live in the 20th century is to wear the stitch of horror on one's heart, so close are we to the edge of violence. This is the time when more than ever we can speak of mass murder, when we fumble for new words like genocide, when the city becomes the home not of the civil man but of the barbarian. Yet, nations and peoples being organized as they are, most of us are physically removed from the violence and normally seem to be uninvolved. We genuinely want peace. We recognize the surgical coldness of a technical age, but we do not consciously want to hate, to hurt, to kill.

If that is the condition of the man of faith, this fifth word seems beside the point. Here more than elsewhere the external disciplines of human law remove temptation. It is a wasteful miscalculation to take someone else's life if the surrender of one's own is the legally inevitable consequence. For death ends the possibilities of both men. Why, then, speak of inner disciplines in relation to the command against killing? If children feel the fourth commanding word to be the most inescapable, will not all of us feel the fifth to be the most escapable?

All this is true until we see how Jesus Christ appropriates the apparently escapable word and pulls it to the inescapable center of His thought. Here is the secret of the hidden discipline: because He was preoccupied with the meaning of belief in His Father and with complete concern for men, it is precisely this kind of command which carries most weight. If in the days of the old covenant the mandate was necessary for the nomad, the warrior, the wandering cutthroat bands, under the new covenant more is to be expected. Not even the word or the desire to kill should be present: even these limit the possibilities of freedom for the other.

We must not kill, either by hand, heart, or word, by signs or gestures. Jesus on the cross experienced how little room the world had for One who had no hate at all in Him; He was edged out of the city, into the suburbs, and up onto a gibbet. He earned the right to intensify the command. "But I say unto you . . ." He could say, and move the emphasis from the killing act to the hateful thought. And in His resurrection He brought into reality a new humanity. He was God's visitation of our race; after He hid the life of men with Himself in God, no man in his private circumstances had the right to take away or regard lightly the life and freedom of another. If he did, he showed lack of faith in God's determining power. If he did, he showed lack of love; God had not *found,* He had *created* the object of His love. Man was to imitate God; man could not reject others who did not fit his mold.

In the first place, we should not harm anyone. This means, first, by hand or by deed; next, we should not use our tongue to advocate or advise harming anyone; again, we should neither use nor sanction any means or methods whereby anyone may be harmed; finally, our heart should harbor no hostility or malice toward anyone in a spirit of anger and hatred. Here a double movement is implied,

from the hand back to the heart, from the heart forward
to the hand.

First, the negative movement, from the hand back to the
heart: the prohibition to kill or hate. He who hates "has
not eternal life." There is no promise here, no indulgence
toward human psychology, no empathy on God's part;
there is only accusation. The old covenant's command not
to kill becomes a parable of the new covenant's urgent
word: do not even limit love. Death ends the possibilities
of a man; so does hate. If I resent, bear a grudge, keep
score, erect barriers against another, neither he nor I am
free to serve. I may use the weapon of words, of petty
actions, of unspoken thoughts. Look at the practical effects:

The world narrows. First there is someone whom I cannot meet. We cannot look each other in the eye; some
of the world's psychic space has been removed. We cannot communicate, for we do not share faith in each other's
real humanness. Neither of us can be at his best, for we
are unnerved. We limit each other as creations. It is in-
conceivable that we can now carry on a pattern of redeeming, of making something of the raw material of the
other's life. We cannot act out the holiness called for
from men of faith. The last stage — which arrives even
without a concrete action's having been undertaken — is
that I wear earmuffs. I can no longer hear the Gospel.
If I hate my brother whom I have seen, how can I love
God, whom I have not seen? God is effectively cut out
of the life of one and possibly two persons. This is why
Jesus was so concerned that a man should leave his gift
at the altar until he had made peace with his brother.
Jesus had faith in the initiative of the forgiving man. He
does not say, Take the gift back home. He suggests that
the forgiver will soon be back at the altar, soon free again
to worship.

You cannot reject the creature to whom God has given
life. You cannot narrow the possibilities for another creature. Even as we hear these words, we have difficulty
picturing anyone who lives up to them. That is exactly

the point: this command, which seemed so escapable, becomes our great accuser. Human relations are not based on the insecure footing of a man's inherent possibilities but on the power inherent in the Word and will of God. Will Rogers' comment, "I never met a man I did not like," may be psychologically fruitful, but it has little theological weight. What if, one day, he did? Did he perhaps have low standards of liking? Something more secure is needed: I never met a man whose life exempted me from seeing him written into this provision of God for that life.

Just as much or more must be made of the positive movement of this word, from the heart forward to the hand. Taking life or hating life is evidence of the unbelieving heart; failing to do good with the hand is evidence of the unimaginative heart. *This commandment is violated not only when a person actually does evil, but also when he fails to do good to his neighbor, or, though he has the opportunity, fails to prevent, protect, and save him from suffering bodily harm or injury. If you send a person away naked when you could clothe him, you have let him freeze to death. . . . It will do you no good to plead that you did not contribute to his death by word or deed, for you have withheld your love from him and robbed him of the service by which his life might have been saved.*

Room is here for a grand vision of man's possibilities. We who wear the stitch of horror on our hearts can also wear the stitch of honor. If this is the generation of genocide, it is also the generation that has another choice. Arnold Toynbee remarks that the 20th century will be chiefly remembered as an age in which human society dared to think of the welfare of the whole human race as a practicable objective. Today the man of faith can use the technical aspects of the modern world, its productivity, its economic outlook, its political order, to enhance what he is to be doing in his own front yard all the time.

Jesus Christ died for all; the word of judgment required active concern for even the least of His brethren. Now man's control of physical means has reached a point where active concern for the all and the least appears workable. The command is inescapable if I understand the gift of life. The Law stabs at me for failing to understand. Do the world's victims of anarchy or authoritarianism know that we would effectuate this love? Are they sustained by our acts and our prayers and by the knowledge of our acceptance of their circumstances? We are not given the choice of taking our signals from the world with its counsels of political, economic, personal expediency. Jesus Christ died for the privilege of forcing His logic of love in the face of the expedient and the prudential. He seeks people capable of recklessness, flamboyant generosity. Their actions can make His hints, His whispers, sound louder than the shouts and the jarring cacophonies of selfishness.

VI

"You shall not commit adultery."

That child did not speak for his culture who observed that since adults did nothing but sit around and talk, nothing was duller than adultery. Preoccupied as it is with the senses, our culture finds adultery a highly attractive subject. A preacher can usually count on a large assembly if he announces that he will chastise in lurid terms the sins that are glamorously organized under the term adultery. If the laws and external disciplines of life help prevent open violations of the Fifth Command, they break down significantly when it comes to the Sixth. Social pressures, laws, conventions tend to relax here, and the hidden disciplines of the forgiven life are doubly necessary.

The dramatic portrayal of the adulterous life does a disservice to the person of faith in that it distracts from the real intentions of the command. In a guidebook to a Western ghost town I read that the quest for the gold which was not there caused miners to overlook the rich silver that was. People who look for the glamor of sins of the flesh are likely to overlook the happiness of the disciplined life. The one threatens never to bring happiness; the other promises always to do so. Billboards, magazines, newsstands, the advertising world to the contrary notwithstanding, there is a durable beauty in a stable relationship built on belief in God and concern for persons as persons. *Inasmuch as there is a shameful means and cesspool of all kinds of vice and lewdness among us, this commandment applies to every form of unchastity, however it is called. Not only is the external act forbidden, but also every kind of cause, motive, and means. Your heart, your lips, and your whole body are to be chaste and to afford no occasion, aid, or encouragement to unchastity. Moreover, you are to defend, protect, and rescue your neighbor whenever he is in danger or need, and on the contrary to aid and assist him so that he may retain his honor. Whenever you fail to do this (though you could prevent a wrong) or wink at it as if it were no concern of yours, you are just as guilty as the culprit himself.*

Once again the issues are between belief and unbelief, between respect for and misuse of creation. First, unbelief: in the Old Testament adultery and idolatry are often closely related. The one makes the forbidden other the object of his worship so that he can break down divinely established disciplines. He places on the other a weight she cannot bear as a creature; he places her on the pedestal along with other household gods. After his desires have displaced God in the desiring one, the act of adultery is merely an expression of a guilt already present. God who forbids adultery is not an executive recommending a different pattern of action, but a judging and loving God. It is the man who does not really hear the Word of God who fails to work at understanding human relations. An unbelieving society places a tremendous strain on the man of faith, sustained only by inner disciplines. When a culture sees marriage as a convenient temporary contract and enacts laws to support this view, it throws the Christian completely on faith in the Word of God.

Sometimes a more vivid way to face the problem posed by unchastity is to observe what it does to the creation, to someone else's personhood. This matter also is related to idolatry; all the commands are related to the first. When man commits adultery, he misuses what God makes. The "I" is related then not to "thou" — a free but responsible other person — but to an "it" which can be used to gratify impulses. "I love you, which means that I love me and you give me pleasure." The erotic emphasis on pinup pictures, the idea of playgirls as a man's accessory — these are evidence that the other has become a thing. The cult of the love goddess or beauty goddess, as a half-serious religion demanding divine seriousness of its devotees, makes of the woman a thing instead of a person. The movement, by the way, can go the other way with equal lack of finesse — female making a thing of the male.

What went wrong when there is adultery? Some personal relation broke down. The breakdown could happen only after one or two or three or more parties were regarded as things. Of course, this turning of persons into things can also occur in marriage, in the name of chastity and high standards. When the one withholds himself, when he is resentful, indifferent, "chaste" without outpouring love, when he keeps score in arguments, he may seem to be operating within the framework of high ethical standards. But he is committing adultery by misusing the creation, by making a thing of his partner for the sake of his ego, his standards, his willfulness.

The Sixth Command is an extension of the Faith, but it calls forth much more of the chosen, responsive, hidden discipline. The commands relating to the neighbor are in logical order: *First they deal with our neighbor's person. Then they proceed to the person nearest and dearest to him, namely, his wife, who is one flesh and blood with him.* If the fifth word involved two in lovelessness, the sixth involves at least three, where marriage is concerned. This

23

form of lovelessness fails to see Christ's kind of love, which looks to the others' needs first. "Christ loved the church and gave Himself for it" is the prototype of marriage. Christ showed a new kind of relation between persons. This change does not liberate people so that merely to assent to it gives one license: even in marriage, *God's grace is still required to keep the heart pure.*

In the time of the Reformation, marriage was downgraded by a church which elevated celibacy and virginity to the highest status. Today marriage is upstaged by a world which elevates license, unbelief, lack of concern for the other, and lovelessness in the name of romantic love. Both settings violate the divine pattern; both call forth a double measure of alertness and discipline. When God is seen as the Giver, as One who cares; when the other is seen as a person, not as a thing; when love is seen as the bridge between humans and not as the euphemism for selfishness, this Sixth Command will find its place as a liberator. Men can find new freedom, new outlets to help others work the works of God in the world of men.

VII

"You shall not steal."

For the Fifth Word society provides an external discipline; the Sixth breaks down such discipline; but in regard to the Seventh, society has embraced a way of life that imposes fracture of the command. If what is here forbidden includes also misrepresentation, false bargaining, shoddy craftsmanship, then it must be said that in some senses the whole economy would collapse if men lived up to this commandment.

Next to our own person and our spouse, our temporal property is dearest to us. This, too, God wants to have protected. . . . This includes taking advantage of our neighbor . . . and relates to people *who are careless and unreliable in their work.* But if the man of faith listens carefully to the sentence "God wants to have our property protected," he can be diverted for a moment from con-science-searching. He is filled with joy at this further evidence of God's love. God gives "all things" with Jesus Christ and preserves them. He gives bodily life, spouse, and, now, possessions.

But as he listens further and learns that God cares about and protects his possessions, the man of faith is moved to ask concerning their meaning. Do they rule him or does he rule them? The question is particularly pertinent for the man who has numbers of possessions. We remember the properties Gandhi left behind: a book, spectacles, sandals; we recall the mythology of the Franciscan legacy — almost no material property. Looking at the well-used objects, we know that they were servants of those who used them, not masters. A worn canehandle or plow handle, a sewing machine or a typewriter, a lived-in house or a lived-in shoe — these are evidence that material objects can serve men.

Is this, we must ask, what I get out of the command? The danger is persistent that we hear only its prohibitions — that we divorce its content from its author. And on this tack we shall miss the real meaning of its prohibitions. For they relate to that part of our property about which we are already confident. Every man has learned "mine" and "thine"; "His" and "Hers" are stamped on the bath-room towels; cash registers, locks on doors, and police forces reveal society's assumptions concerning its members. But one can hardly see the command in the light of the Christian faith if one stops at locks and policemen.

With all the commands the fact is that, when one is con-fident that he has plumbed the meaning of a command and can safely evade it, its most profound meaning must be eluding him. The task here must be to see why God concerns Himself with the property of men.

What is forbidden is open, obvious stealing; for the good of the neighbor the prohibition is necessary. It has nothing to do with the respectable member of society, it would seem — until we note that tens and hundreds of millions of dollars in the national economy are written into the overhead of supermarket owners who deal only with the respectables. Secondly, taking advantage of the other is forbidden. This is a more difficult situation for the man of conscience as he examines an expense-account society which plans obsolescence into its products. Even politics enters here. If one is conservative about economics, he shouts "welfare state" at all who would see to it that the poor are well regarded; if he is a liberal, he will shout "exploitation" at all who want to build personal incentives into the economy. If he is a laborer, he will point to the conniving of management; if he is a manager, he will point to the stealing written into the structure of big labor. All can find excuse: these structures seem too big for the individual to have an impact on them.

While the excuse-making goes on one is likely once again to overlook the profound meanings in the command. In the root of our evasions and excuses, here as with all the other commands lie unbelief, the pursuit of false gods, slavery to creatures, to possessions. The issue then is not: Whose materialism: communism's or capitalism's? Who is right, the liberal or the conservative? The issue is God's ownership and man's stewardship. God has His monogram on my possessions; I am to use them for others. This leads to the positive side of the Seventh Command.

We are commanded to promote and further our neighbor's interests, and when he suffers want, we are to help, share, and lend to both friends and foes. The one who fails to help is in a most serious situation. If the oppressed man cries to heaven, *such a man's sighs and cries will be no joking matter. They will have an effect too heavy for you and all the world to bear, for they will reach God, who watches over poor, sorrowful hearts, and He will not leave them unavenged.*

How does one reverse such a terrifying process? First, he must hear the word of judgment in its sharpness and

severity. Second, if he believes, he will take its seriousness seriously. Third, he will recognize in the providing
hand of God the source of his gifts. Fourth, he will know
that determination of the use to which these gifts shall
be put belongs to God, who permits no careless, lazy understanding. Fifth, he will look to the need of the other,
not gaining status by rejoicing in his own good fortune in
comparison with others' misfortunes. Sixth, he will know
that someone must take a stand; the power structures of
national life are ordinarily made up of men more than half
of whom profess Christianity — is there no power to reverse
trends there? Seventh, he will learn a judicious use of the
resources God places in the earth. Eighth, he will teach
the young to rectify the mistakes of the previous generation.
Ninth, he will look at the cross and see in the renunciation
it symbolizes the kind of freedom from things which makes
men free to appreciate things.

So the attitude to possessions becomes one more test of
God's Lordship, belief in Christ's Sonship, and the concern
for the neighbor. "Mine" and "thine" are both written
over the "His" that signifies the rightful owner. And He
will not be denied His own way, His own right, His own
opportunity to care for others.

VIII

"You shall not bear false witness against your neighbor."

As each command is heard, as if for the thousandth time,
it is likely to be dismissed as an occasion for moralizing.
The fifth command gives the moralizer occasion for the
tremendously subtle observation that one can kill without
a sword. What is new there? The sixth evokes comment
on the low quality of magazines today. Anyone could note
that, without criteria established by Christianity. The
seventh command? Yes, we are aware of dimestore pilfer-
ing. The eighth? The moralizer demonstrates how in-

ventive he is by pointing out that not only the courtroom
but also the backyard fence is involved. And every time
such casual utterances rule out the seriousness of the command, something happens. The radical, tight, tense, taut
character of the divine command is left behind. Issues
of unbelief and the meaning of persons can be skimmed
over.

What is actually involved in this command? A first step
toward an answer is to dramatize the meaning of personhood. Fix in your mind any person of slight acquaintance,
perhaps someone you have only seen but do not know.
Now ask what it is that his personhood represents. The
immediate answer would certainly be, "Not much" — a
name in a phonebook, a time of seventy years, a place that
will be obliterated so that the winds over the fields will
know it no more. But he has been given the gift of life.
Now imagine the rest. He knows that living is difficult.
No doubt he wipes children's noses, brings home paychecks,
laughs, cries. He has no high aspirations; maybe he hopes
his children can go to college. He likes a good dinner;
often he likes to be left alone. He may be religious and
even a man in Christ. He hopes. He feels a lump in his
throat and freezes with horor at the thought that it might
be cancer. He shines his shoes. He will die, and he is
afraid of death, or at least it is a cloud across his life. He
has a thousand little comforts and joys that mean little
to anyone else. And he has a name. It represents his integrity, his personhood; it may be all that he has to
trade on.

It is in your power to rob him of it.

*We have one more treasure which is indispensable to us,
namely our honor and good name. . . . Therefore God will
not have our neighbor deprived of his reputation, honor,
and character.*

The name may have been accidentally applied to him;
it may be absurd, atonal, nonsensical. But it implies an
integrity, a whole person. One can scramble and scrabble
the letters, play games with it acoustically. W-n-a-g-e: no

harm done. Agnew: a whole constellation of thoughts comes to mind. E-r-m-n-o-o and Monroe; L-l-t-m-h-c-i-e and Mitchell; as soon as sense is made of letters and sound waves, a reputation is at stake.

If that reputation lies in my power to break or to make, I must see it in its Christian dimension. I can cut off a man's creative possibility; I can seem to stand in the way of the Word that would redeem him; I can rob him of motives for holiness. I can do this by my word and by my silence.

Most of this is common sense. The hidden discipline of the forgiven life comes into play when I look at him from the viewpoint of Jesus Christ on the cross. Now the man appears in a new light. He was given a name at creation: Adam, man. At baptism he was given a new name: the new man. It is said of him that he shall see things greater than any that kings desired to see or ever saw. He takes part in a Supper which prefigures a heavenly banquet. God Himself did not count the cost when it came to incorporating this solitary one into His plan. This man did not deserve the attention: he blasphemed, he spat, he bore false witness against Jesus in His hour of aloneness (". . . you have done it unto Me . . ."). But Jesus bore the injustice from him to win him back. It is impossible to picture Jesus Christ, the great Confronter, discussing the man behind his back.

Jesus, as a matter of fact, took a stand and always takes a stand with the victimized. He stands behind Iron Curtains and in slums and juvenile courts. He is described as representative and go-between. He is condemned whenever generalizations are made which limit personal integrity: "Catholics are . . . ." "Irish always . . . ." "Negroes usually . . . ." "Baptists are known to . . . ." "Slum dwellers never . . . ." And He stands among them. But if I see myself condemned as I make the generalizations and bear the false witness, so I am saved as I see Him range Himself with me when I am put upon; He restores my name with the grace of His own.

The man of faith thus sees the neighbor with the eye of

both humaneness and the hidden concern of Jesus Christ. The gift of a name is the one more treasure wrapped up in God. God will not have the neighbor deprived of it; He sets up governments, courts of justice, laws to protect it. And when these fail, the church must be free to stand with Jesus Christ. (Is it free?) Meanwhile, when the man of faith is put upon, he must not issue direct reply. He must turn his destiny over to God. Nor is he to rejoice in misfortunes relating to another's name; he is involved.

When you become aware of a sin, simply make your ears a tomb and bury it until you are appointed a judge. To do otherwise is unbelief, the assertion of God's impotence to rule and rectify, *it is nothing else than usurping the judgment and office of God.* The busybody is the idolater, making a false god of himself.

New Year's resolutions are of little effect compared with the perspective to be gained from taking seriously a divine command. Then one can put himself through the paces:

If one sins against this command, he is showing that he is frustrated, insecure, inferior. He must elevate himself at the expense of at least one other human. All others know this of him and he knows it of all others but not of himself.

If he sins against this command, he shows that he disbelieves God's power to judge and to establish orders of justice in which the man of faith can participate to correct injustices.

If his ears are stopped to this command, he shows that it has not occurred to him that Christ came to stake a stand with the name that is being misused.

If he violates its intention, he reveals that he does not understand the resurrection and the new creation which gives every name a new beginning.

If he goes against this command, he ranges himself against Christ and sees Christ range Himself against the offender and not with him.

If he violates it, he shows that he has not learned the hidden discipline of wanting the best for the other who is also forgiven.

Jesus tells us of a different pattern. *"If he listens to you,"* this man against whose name you have something, *"you have gained your brother."* *Then you have done a great and excellent work. Do you think it is an insignificant thing to gain a brother? Let all monks and holy orders step forth, with all their works heaped up together, and see if they can make the boast that they have gained one brother!*

IX · X

"You shall not covet."

The commands can be seen concentrically. At the center is a concern for God's claim on the life of man — the first three commands. The fourth sets up the relations of man to man in permanent structures. The fifth begins with the situation of having and holding life within these structures; the sixth speaks of the nearest and dearest; the seventh of a regard for possessions — the semidetached part of man. The eighth intervenes to reinforce the others. The last two in combination are concerned with the outermost circle: the unspoken, unaccomplished, unenacted desire for the possessions of another. At this point several observations are in order.

First, this command suggests that the passing of centuries does bring somewhat different circumstances to interpretation. In the open, nomadic, unpoliced society the sinful desire for someone else's possessions could readily be transformed into action appropriating them. A more sophisticated society provides legal though not always more humane measures for appropriating another's property.

Second, this command surprises us in that it seems unnecessary to preserve human society. Hence it suggests the theological or Godward dimensions of the Law. The Law is not just a handy little guide for the moral life, a good scouts' handbook. It serves to accuse the person who claims uprightness before God. God reaches into the recesses of the heart where the springs of human interaction are concealed. The Law is therefore no path to new life; salvation is not the same as the hidden discipline of the forgiven man who makes no claim upon God.

Third, what is seen so profoundly in the Sermon on the Mount is made evident in this command: that the sinful desire is, from God's side, as evil as the act. For it is based on the root sin of unbelief: it asserts that God does not know how to order and distribute possessions and people. It shows lack of concern for the neighbor, implying that the desiring one had more right to possessions. *Such is nature that we all begrudge another's having as much as we have.*

Fourth, the hidden character of the Christian ethic is made evident here where action is not involved. It is the character of the forgiven heart that is called into question; the external code is unimportant by comparison.

Finally, as Paul reminds us when he speaks the accusing character of the Law under which he "died," this command accuses where man had not seen wrong. Paul avers that by conscience and experience he would not even have known that to covet was to transgress; he had to hear the command to become aware of this sin. This means that the Law is beamed especially to the religious man: *This last commandment, then, is addressed not to those whom the world considers wicked rogues, but precisely to the most upright* — to people who wish to be commended as honest and virtuous because they have not offended against the preceding commandments. ... *This commandment remains, like all the rest, one that constantly accuses us and shows just how upright we really are in God's sight.*

The Law accuses; it does not save. In this command its inadequacy as a path to the forgiven life is plainly revealed. How radical is God's concern to act both in His wrath and in His love is made clear in the next word, associated preeminently with His first word of command.

The man who mines diamonds will also be exposing to the world new specks of carbon. The man who mines in the Word of God will ordinarily be attracted by its light and its brilliance. Occasionally he will come across what looks like an imperfection, a carbon speck, a black spot, a shadow which immediately stands out against the background. Its blackness will exaggerate itself and obscure the brilliance. This will certainly be the experience of anyone who takes seriously the word appended to the First Command and often studied as a sequel to all the Ten Commands:

"I, the Lord, your God, am a jealous God, visiting the iniquity of the fathers upon the children to the third and fourth generation of them that hate Me."

That is the first half of the sentence. While it will be outshone by the promise of the second half, it is not nonsense. It is a clear, definable, deliberate statement. It was not rattled off casually, jotted down carelessly, neglectfully preserved. It has to be taken seriously.

Reflective people will find it difficult so to take it, whether the picture of God they carry in their heart has been inadequate or adequate. This picture drawn in this statement counters all the popular portraits of God. As an instance: the man who noisily or carelessly declares that God is dead is saying that everything is permissible, that "all is grace." Such a man cannot take seriously the word of a "jealous" God. On the other hand, listening to the word in an evangelical church may lead him to a similar conclusion. God is grace, and God is all, therefore *God* is grace. Grace is a marketplace item, available to the low bidder. The one who has faith in Jesus Christ is described as possessing grace; who then can lay requirements upon him? For he does not live under the Law. So, whether God is dead or whether God is grace, man is ill equipped to take seriously the word of a God who describes Himself as being jealous.

How un-American this God! We had defined the God of the Bible in the comfortable terms we like today. We had put Him on the shelf with other household gods, polished Him up, wrapped and packaged Him, and drawn security from the fact that He met our terms. He loves everyone; He dotes on all His children.

But a "jealous" God? We seek explanations. The first that comes to mind would ascribe this term to old and outworn views of His self-revelation. Some would call it anthropomorphism — the attempt to hang on to God all the vices and virtues of men and then blow them up to divine size. That this is not the best answer is clear from the fact that on all levels and planes of the sacred Scripture God depicts Himself as capable of showing wrath as well as love. His jealousy does not go away.

This jealousy, of course, is not the same as that which is intolerable in human relations. It preserves what is right about such human jealousy: that it is based in part on great interest in the other. But human jealousy is also based on insecurity; it is a blinding emotion that rules out other concerns. Every relation of God to His people refutes this picture.

Throughout His old covenant God is entering into relations with His people. This is clear above all in the prophecy of Hosea, where Israel's unfaithfulness to God is portrayed by the harlot wife's unfaithfulness to her husband. In the same book a parent-child relation between God and His people is depicted. What is important in these pictures is that when God reveals Himself, He does not set forth a literal code, ten easy (or hard) lessons in being a follower. He establishes a personal relation, a bond; He suffers with His creature and rejoices with him or her. "Jealousy" is the term that covers the ultimate seriousness with which God would guard the relation. A complete case against the faith could be based on the misreading or isolating of this one text.

The next phrase is perhaps even more offensive: that God visits the evil of the fathers upon the children to the third and fourth generation of those that hate Him. This surely is unworthy of God, whose Fatherhood is to be a model for earthly fathers. But — in passing — is it not ironic that these words are least understood and most mistrusted by the first human generation which has seen them become true even on the natural level? As the world crowds up and its resources are exploited and wasted, the fathers' sins will be visited upon the children. As nuclear weapons spread radioactive debris to disturb the genetic apparatus, defects will appear in children and grandchildren. Thus the natural principle of the continuing consequences of any generation's acts is made graphic. But let us not use the natural picture to take the strain off this offensive note. First, some questions as to its earnestness.

The man of faith must ask whether, before he tries to tone down the severity of this note of God's wrath, he has taken God seriously. Has he permitted God to be God? Or has he manufactured a human picture of God, an idol, a mold into which he can pour the divine revelation? Has he thought seriously what would happen to him if God's freedom is lost so that God cannot act as He will? Has he considered what his emphasis on God's grace, apart from God's wrath, would do to the wholeness of the revelation?

Second, he must ask, with St. Anselm of long ago, whether he has taken sin with its full seriousness and thought what it does to the bond between God and man and between man and man. Can man take sin seriously if he conceives of God as an overblown man in his dotage, rocking away in an upstairs apartment and tending flowerpots in his spare time?

Third, has he taken seriously the weight his own personal sin lays upon him? Not at all does this mean that the faith expects man to run around with hangdog mien, bewailing his wrongdoings and shortcomings. Rather it recognizes the anguish which the misspent day, the harsh word or deed, the disrupted relation brings to a man who takes life and love seriously. This experience can be creative only if God's grace is taken seriously against the pattern of what is here called His "jealousy."

Fourth, has he considered that faith in God, this God, has been sustained in the old and new covenants in full awareness of this revelation? Everyone, somewhere in his life, realizes how weighty a fact this is. Would a bond with the divine be formed if people through the long pull of the centuries felt that the religious professionals and bookkeepers were taking polls and drawing up statistics to determine what kind of God people would like on the shelf, and then produced and packaged him? Here the raw, the angular, the disjointed aspect of God's revelation is a reassurance to the man who wants to assess the truth of a word proclaimed.

Fifth, does the man of faith who wants to dismiss this word lightly think of his solidarity, his involvement in the sin of all men, all generations? In a wealthy suburban church he may join his minister in criticizing juvenile delinquency in the city. At the same time he may own the slum apartments which help produce deliquency. Or at least he is not working to change the society which produces it. He rants at the malice in the Russian's heart and is himself filled with petty jealousies. He spends good hours and dollars on a psychiatrist's couch trying to rid himself of the unhappy aftereffects of childhood experiences but makes no effort to deal wisely with his own child, who, victimized by the parents' religious neglect and selfishness, is already visited by the iniquity of the father.

Sixth, has he asked about the self-destructive character of sin? Has he seen what it does to the parents and children who disintegrate in its presence, who see the meaning of life ebb away?

Then comes the turn in the road toward the second half of the sentence, which has not yet been quoted.

Has he, seventh, related what this word says about God to all the rest of the Bible's revelation? Is he isolating the word "jealous," cutting it out of its own sentence, putting it on a billboard, barricading a road with it? Will he wait to hear the other, more dramatic half of the sentence, and will he then see that his chief problem is to relate the offensive word to that second half, and not the other way around?

Eighth, have these words brought home to him the limits of commands and laws as a way to life with God? Who will stand before the One who speaks this word and exempt himself from involvement in the flow of generations?

Last, has he seen this word as a preparation for the good news? Has his focus on the carbon made him familiar with the dazzle of the diamond that surrounds it?

These questions serve to throw against a larger screen the problem each man faces when he does not take the word seriously.

What is here called iniquity is always exposed as such against the background of a command of God. Man measures, sometimes consciously and sometimes casually, whether or not to obey. If he sets out on a path of disobedience, he soothes himself by seeking company. The company he finds helps him enjoy the wrong but cannot help him make creative use of the misfortune or guilt that comes later. He seeks excuses. The relation of trust has been destroyed.

Man comes to a dead end.

Here is where God picks up the pieces; here is the decisive turn in our narrative of the hidden discipline. Listening to the second half of the sentence becomes a fresh experience: *"I, the Lord, your God . . . to those who love and keep My commandments . . . show mercy unto a thousand generations."* If before there was concern that old Oriental expressions and anthropomorphisms might obscure a divine word, now we welcome old Oriental ways of putting things. Call it the exaggeration of contrast: better, it is a statement of fact. God measures out in a ratio of 250 to one, of 333-1/3 to one, and more, His mercy to those who love Him. He had called a wandering tribesman to head His people; He had led a people out of slavery and through a desert; He had given them kings and prophets; He gives them a hope, a promise, a Son. He had once asked man to count the stars in order to know the number of the promises, to scan the heavens with the arc of his eye in order to measure the rainbow of promise; now He asks them to look at His mercy in Jesus Christ.

Later on, when Jesus spoke, He was not heard either in the mode men expected. There was little of the saccharine or the sentimental, little relaxing of discipline in His own discourse. He used hard words, stressing the enormousness of God's demands on men. In His presence man also dead-ended: "Who then can be saved?" In His presence the new creation began: "With men this is impossible; with God all things are possible."

Jesus is not remembered for the hard words that threw men on the promises of God. He is remembered for mirroring the loving heart of His Father. We are invited to reread the word about the jealous God after we have seen the face and form of Jesus on the cross: "He that has seen Me has seen the Father." Jesus was not the son of a father who like an Oriental despot destroyed people at whim and who watched his creatures tumble like puppies at his feet. Jesus grieved over the city and the social solidarity of its sin; he mourned for the daughters of Jerusalem who brought evil on their children. He expended His breath and pulse and life to the last to be identified with those whose iniquity brought out God's wrath, whose love grew in response to God's thousand-generationed mercy.

Whether or not the world that stands outside the covenant is attracted by the word of God's jealousy is less important than the fact that the word is heard once again within. God does not tolerate presumption; He does not permit men to stomp with dirty boots across the lives of others. But He identifies Himself with man in his need: "He has made Jesus to be sin for us," Him who "knew no sin." At last we have seen a man, the man for the thousand generations.

These words contain both a wrathful threat and a friendly promise, not only to terrify and warn us but also to attract and allure us. These words, therefore, ought to be received and esteemed as a serious matter to God because He Himself here declares how important the command-

ments are to Him and how strictly He will watch over them. . . . Thus He demands that all our actions proceed from a heart that fears and regards God alone and, because of this fear, avoids all that is contrary to His will, lest He be moved to wrath; and, conversely, trusts Him alone and for His sake does all that He asks of us, because He shows Himself a kind Father and offers us every grace and blessing.

THE APOSTLES' FAITH, OR CREED

I

Thus far we have heard the first part of Christian doctrine. In it we have seen all that God wishes us to do or not to do. The Creed properly follows, setting forth all that we must expect and receive from God; in brief, it teaches us to know Him perfectly. It is given in order to help us do what the Ten Commandments require of us. . . . If we could by our own strength keep the Ten Commandments as they ought to be kept, we would need neither the Creed nor the Lord's Prayer.

The external discipline of man is based on the code of law, viewed as a letter; on the law of the church, viewed as divine; on the law of custom, ethos, or social pressure, viewed as binding. The hidden discipline is based on belief in God and concern for the neighbor. That belief is summarized in the ancient creed; and to provide the base for the hidden discipline, it is necessary to reexplore the articles of faith as we note *how few people believe [these articles]. We all pass over [them], hear [them] and recite [them], but we neither see nor consider what the words enjoin on us."*

"I believe in God the Father Almighty. . . ." Since the Ten Commandments have explained that we are to have no more than one God, it may be asked: *"What kind of being is God? What does He do? How can we praise or portray or describe Him in such a way as to make Him known?"*

The first word of faith throws together two words: "Father," "Almighty."

This combination is very natural. *But is it? If you were to ask a young child, "My boy, what kind of God have you? What do you know about Him?" he could say, "First, my God is the Father who made heaven and earth."* He could say this if he were preconditioned by the Biblical faith and the culture in which it has been held. But is it natural, obvious, or logical to begin with the assertion about an almighty Father? The boy has been told that it is; his answer is a reflecting, mirroring one. He has been nurtured at the bosom of mother church and so can speak about his Father.

Careful thought based on the normal evidences of lives would, without the preconditioning, come up with many other kinds of answers. Repetition, reminiscence, recall — these make it possible for us to link the two words. But they are not a natural combination. The man who wants to invent a religion would do well to avoid this combination; it is filled with logical difficulties. "Almighty" elevates God; "Father" brings Him down. "Almighty" signifies God's otherness, aloofness, remoteness, self-containedness; "Father" stands for His nearness, His concern, His involvement, His self-emptying love.

"Father" — separate this word from its partner, and difficulties dissolve. By itself this will do as our culture's affirmation about God. It permits us to put God back on grandfather's rocker. (Have those who sing the popular songs and repeat the popular slogans ever noted that the first article of faith does not say, "I believe in the Grandfather almighty"?) "Father" — let it stand by itself, as many religions allow it to do, and matters are simple.

Sigmund Freud saw this idea of God as Father to be the most profound, most explainable, most psychologically appealing part of the Christian faith. Man, thrown out into a cold world which forces decision on him, projects a father image and invents a God who is father. A whole swarm of social psychologists have followed in Freud's path, suggesting that the quest for a father is all that is involved in Christianity. It seems surprising that they should make such a statement when one remembers the rich and contradictory varieties of Christian proclamation through the centuries. At the same time, the fact that such men have pointed to the psychological need for a divine Father ought not frighten the believer, ought not cause him to shy away, to roll over and play dead. God, who would draw man to Himself, knew a thing or two about human psychology and didn't wait for the late nineteenth century to reveal this need for a father.

Most religions would have said that God is Father, naturally. Not so with the people of the Old Covenant and, even more, with the Christian believer. God was not naturally Father; He revealed Himself to be one; Jesus opened the heart of God to reveal its fatherly character. God the Father becomes Father in a new creation: this is seen in the story of the Prodigal Son. "This my son was dead, and is alive again; he was lost, and is found."

"Almighty." — Again, how natural this sounds. It is not a unique and it is not a new assertion in Biblical faith. Many religions point to almighty deities. What amazes the listener to the word "almighty" is the absence in the Bible of any attempt at proving, to say nothing of asserting, that the Father is Almighty. That He is so was not just a proposition, a nice little truth about God; it was assumed as the living reality of God. While other religions aspired to the vision of almightiness, the Bible strains to show God's weakness, His condescension. Sometimes a shocking inversion of the business of proofs is in order. One of the more delicious of these comes from the pen of the late Herbert Kelly, founder of the Society of the Sacred Mission, Kelham (In *The Gospel of God,* S. C. M., 1959, p. 132). The eccentric but profound and witty Anglican recalls:

A very dear old Father visited us from America and I said to him: "Come, and I will show you my proofs of the existence of God." (What I actually said was my "proofs of the Resurrection." . . .) Then I showed him our pigs. I love pigs. They are so delightfully ugly, and so blissfully self-satisfied over it. A fat old sow came slowly waddling toward us, with its two huge ears — like Macbeth's dagger — pointing the way that she would go. And the good Father looked puzzled. "Oh, yes," I replied, "if I had shown you stars, flowers, a sunset, you would have said, 'Ah! how true!' but I do not greatly need God in order to see that beautiful things are beautiful, and — well —

elevating. I do want to hear of a God who can find a
beauty and a joy and an eternal value in my poor pigs.
If God also laughs softly over their funniness, I do not
mind that. I do it too."

God who lets His almightiness be examined in His Fatherhood, in the sunset, and in Father Kelly's pigs — this picture
forces the unnaturalness of the creedal combination on us.

Recent religious impulses have distracted people from
facing up to this particular question of belief. The con-
temporary accent is often obsessed with man in the act
of praying, of being worshipful. So long as the accent falls
on man in the mirror, no decision is forced upon anyone;
it goes unnoticed *how few people believe this article,* and
therefore small energies are poured into building up the
belief of the many. The life with a hidden discipline
devotes itself intensely to exploring all the surprises of
this belief, from the majesty of God to Father Kelly's pigs.

Five aspects of the fatherly almightiness or almighty
fatherliness stand out. First, *the Father . . . daily guards
and defends us against every evil and misfortune, warding
off all sorts of danger and disaster.* It is important to locate
this "warding off." The accounts of Job among his friends
and of Jesus in the garden forbid superficial and magical
views. The believer is never for a moment deceived into
believing that this faith offers him exemption from death.
It does not say he will not get sick, have doubt, verge on
despair, cry out in pain, neglect God and his own solemn
vows, find life easy. It does not license religious professionals to run around sticking labels with facile explanations on the many mysterious aspects of humanity. It
promises but one thing: "Your heavenly Father knows
[your] need." It reinforces this one promise from the
human side: "For I am sure that neither death nor life nor
angels nor principalities nor things present nor things to
come nor powers nor height nor depth nor anything else
in all creation will be able to separate us from the love of
God in Christ Jesus, our Lord" (Rom. 8:38 f.). On this front
— of death and of all creation — God wards off all danger

and disaster. The Christian enters life in the world with his eyes wide open.

Second, *all this [the almighty Father] does out of pure love and goodness, without our merit, as a kind father who cares for us.* This love gives the hidden character to the discipline of life; it is heart, core, and center, the generating impulse. It provides the security and the dash and daring. God did not have to ward off evil. He chose to. He did it not because He came across man as an object worthy of His love. He created man as a subject whom He chose to love. The security in man's relation to God is not based on man's merit. The security resides in God's own character, in His love and goodness. God takes the initiative in Christ. He was in Christ, reconciling the world unto Himself. Therewith He takes His stand against other gods, who are dependent first on the projections, inventions, and aspirations of man.

Third, and in some ways most radical: God comes as Father Almighty not through a set of logical arguments that drop from His mind and mouth and permit Him to contain Himself. *For here we see how the Father has given Himself to us, with all His creatures.* This is not natural, this portrayal of a self-emptying God. It costs God nothing to share sets of proofs or witnesses to His existence. But man's soul is athirst for God, not for proofs of God's existence or character; man seeks a person, not things. Giving of one's self costs. And God's giving of Himself is the convincing center of Christianity. No doubt one can conceive of a God who creates robots that bend to His will. He chose to make men with hearts. The heart cannot be coerced, forced. It must be wooed and won. This is the clue to God's victory in Jesus Christ; He comes from below, to win; not from above, to overpower, awe, and annihilate.

Fourth, response to the loving and self-giving character of the Father claims the energies of the children of God. His treasures are eternal; getting acquainted with Him is worth the effort. He *has showered us with inexpressible eternal treasures through His Son and the Holy Spirit.*

That eternalness does not pull man off to the clouds, out of time and space and this-worldliness. God chooses to sink His hearing in the deafness of mortals, to drench His Word in the agonies of the man of His choosing, to regale man with the panoply of His glories in the middle of this life. The Fourth Gospel shows again and again how eternal life has begun. But God's purposes are not exhausted when the hourglass of history runs out. In the middle of this life His adopted children will do well to become acquainted with the treasure of His love and self-giving. They are not the neighbor's children; they are learning the hidden disciplines of the household where they now belong.

Fifth, the belief brings responsibility. *Therefore this article would humble and terrify us all if we believed it.* Its unnaturalness has been safely codified and shelved so that it cannot easily work its startling power. But if we listen . . . .

The faith begins then with the assertion "I believe in . . . ." The end of man and the birth of the new man are seen in it. He was lost and is found by the Almighty. Even more, he was dead and is alive; thus the Father of Jesus Christ and his own Father sees him.

Oh, yes, the hidden discipline of this love also reminds him: If I have,a Father, and He has other sons, they are my brothers.

The other combination in the first article of faith is apparently equally unnatural: "*I believe in God the Father Almighty, Maker . . .*" Once again, most people would naturally say that naturally there is a creator, a force, a being, an energy that produces the material world. But it is not natural to assert that the almighty Father involves Himself in creating and sustaining the order of things surrounding man and, most of all, man himself. Belief in God the Creator? That is nothing much. "Everyone" has it. Back to the little boy who could answer the question "*What kind of God have you?*" with the words, "*First, my God is the Father, who made heaven and earth. Apart from*

45

Him alone I have no other God, for there is no one else who could create heaven and earth."

Once again, the boy is preconditioned, speaking from within the covenant, from within the faith. That some force or energy stands behind other forces and energies: that is natural. That God the Father of Jesus Christ makes me, that is something else. This personal involvement is startling, almost offensive when one pictures space in its penultimately infinite expansions. Is not this another of the evidences that Dr. Freud has a point or two, that my ego places me at the center of things and the worlds must swirl around my orbit?

Yes, this may be startling and offensive. But, while the Bible takes enough pains to separate God's creating ways from man's reason and responses (see Job 38 and 39), it also personalizes the whole activity "from my mother's womb."

The Genesis narratives must be seen in this light. Read them carefully. They do not begin with a scientific inquiry, "How did the worlds come into being? God created them." Rather they begin with a personal or an historical question: "From what source does the activity of God's people derive its meaning and substance?" The answer: from its origin and sustenance in God. This makes all the difference. Then one sings less blithely the tributes to someone in the great somewhere, hymns celebrating creation in the flower, the newborn baby. Then one inquires with less scientific zeal at what time of the day 6,000 years ago God said, "Let there be . . ."

Instead the Bible turns from natural explanations and natural sciences, turns even beyond history, to personal history to permit man to say: *I hold and believe that I am a creature of God; . . .* none of us has his life of himself . . . *nor can he by himself preserve [it].* Ordinarily people see the movement from an impersonal creator to a divine Father; more correctly, the creed asserts a movement from the Father Almighty to Creatorship. It begins not with deductions about the world but with a word about the

Word. The creedal word is spoken because God has spoken
first in the creation of light and because He has let this
light shine out of darkness into man's heart in the face
and form of Jesus Christ (2 Cor. 5). "By the word of
the Lord were the heavens made." Not: "There is a world,
there must have been a Word." God acts, He initiates, He
moves spontaneously. Only through the divine paternity
of Christ am I moved to find the Creator.

If the initiative is placed with God's action, here again
man is liberating himself to live the life of hidden discipline.
He is not thrown into anxious questioning about proofs of
God's existence or the restrictions imposed on his own
finitude. He is ready out of this first great assertion of
faith, this spark across the infinite nights of separation,
to see God's freedom and his own new possibilities. Then
the birth of one child, of one painting, one song, one flower
serves to enlarge upon a creation that is already affirmed;
it does not substantiate the existence of someone in the
great somewhere.

The test of this belief comes in the crises of life: at
the yawning, gaping graveside one asks, "Did this life
matter?" But the test comes more frequently in the small
meanings and obscure unfoldings of daily life on the
125,000 working days of people in the 24,000 kinds of
vocations our society has to offer.

> Take away our clothes, our food, our liquor, our quaint
> sexual pleasures, our fatiguing little conversations and our
> loathesome excitements about this and that: what's left?
> A hollow thing, like one of those silver Christmas-tree
> ornaments, with no more blood or warmth . . . nothing's
> left because we never really believed anything, we never
> rose above the world of objects, we never deep down
> within us were alive. (A character in Fredric Prokosch's
> novel *The Asiatics*.)

Is it not strange that men could come home from what
looked like a meaningless war and say they found meaning
there more readily than in laboring or in executing details
of prosperous life? Is it not a matter of uncommon interest

that a mother who despairs in her boredom on the days when all goes well and when all lies in her hands, suddenly lays hold of a vivid faith in her Creator in a crisis, when a child is deathly ill? The practical details of living reveal the presence of God, but taken in tedious sequence they have a deadening effect. Without contemplation, or nourishment, the presence is cheapened and then forgotten.

This is why Biblical faith asserts the distinctiveness and separatedness of the Father who is Creator, who then relates Himself to the creature. God has taken the Christian and hidden his life in Jesus Christ. *None of us has his life of himself.* The man who learns this learns that this is not strange: it is consistent with the character of *the Father Almighty,* Maker to continue His creative acts by participating in the new freedom of the new creature.

II

"And in Jesus Christ, His only Son, our Lord . . ."

When we were created by God the Father, and had received from Him all kinds of good things, the devil came and led us into disobedience, sin, death, and all evil. We lay under God's wrath and displeasure, doomed to eternal damnation, as we had deserved. There was no counsel, no help, no comfort for us until this only and eternal Son of God, in His unfathomable goodness, had mercy on our misery and wretchedness and came from heaven to help us. Those tyrants and jailers now have been routed, and their place has been taken by Jesus Christ, the Lord of life and righteousness and every good and blessing.

This discussion of the hidden discipline of the Christian life is not and does not set out to be a full-range and systematic examination of Christian teaching. If it followed this traditional line, the present section with its witness to Christ's Lordship and redeeming activity would occupy a large percentage of the space. Instead Christ's work is the undertone in all the discussions. Rather than attempt to do partial justice to so complicated a topic we shall content ourselves with hooking into our consciousness but two ideas: Christ's Lordship, and what it means that the man Jesus redeems.

Lordship. The Lordship of Jesus Christ is celebrated constantly. The Christian recognizes it as he affirms his Baptism daily on arising. The liturgies of the Holy Communion show forth "the Lord's" death until He comes. The term is mouthed whenever a Christian confesses. It may seem gratuitous therefore to pause for a moment to discuss something so obvious. Who is curious? What Christian has a problem with the reality? Is not the case here a bit like that of the famed research specialist who invented a cure for a disease that did not yet exist? Is a discussion of Lordship not just a hollow attempt at answering a nonexistent question? Is there any doubt about the Lordship inside the community of Jesus Christ (or about the decisiveness of its rejection outside the community)?

But the creed takes the question away from the realms of dogma and liturgy and turns to personal life: it asks, "Has your life a Lord? Is Christ your Lord? Does the answer make a difference?" To assert the Lordship implies first of all that Christ comes from beyond the ordinary stuff out of which human limitations emerge; He comes into our order. He comes, and then *becomes my Lord.* There was little that was natural about the process, though the process moves amid the ordinariness of the natural: the birth of a baby, the walking of Palestinian paths, the death of a man outside Jerusalem, His triumph in men's hearts.

Should he triumph? Ought not the first question to be: should a man have a Lord? Eric Hoffer has written chillingly of the true believer, "the man who looks for Lords, for Fuehrers; who escapes from freedom to be dominated by the earthly lordly." Can it be said that we need more of this? Is it not true that we need less of it, that we must fashion a more responsible freedom in a lordless world?

The answer will issue from the answer to the question "What kind of Lord is Jesus Christ?" Does He want to vanquish the heart of man or woo it? Does He want to overpower and annihilate or to win and keep?

The man of faith, or the man who considers himself a man of faith, begins then by asking whether his life has a Lord. Having thought through the First Commandment of God, a man may presume he has a Lord, whether his reference be to the true God or not. That to which man turns is his God; but even the little gods men erect may not be Lords. They may by their nature be anti-Lords, may help produce vacuums in human existence. When a man is captive to evil, his life does not have the personal organizing center: *Before this I had no Lord and King but was captive*. A lordless life means a chaotic, drifting, aimless life; it is into this kind of life that Fuehrers and fanatics can make their way. *Before this I had no Lord;* my gods crumbled when I touched them. My political party, my integrity, my view of world affairs; my husband, my job, my good name — these were too fragile to hold a life together.

But now! Now the confessing Christian says he has a Lord: *I believe that Jesus Christ, true Son of God, has become my Lord.* "Kyrios Christos." Christ is the Lord.

Every new look down history's corridors, every attempt to poke under the archaeological rubble of the earliest liturgies, points to the primitiveness of this confession. The first thing — and the last and most encompassing — that the man of faith says and can say is that Jesus is his Lord. This is an intensely monotheistic confession; it cannot be seen as an opening statement that leads toward the introduction of witness to any number of gods. Indeed, it is the complete check that forecloses and prevents witness to a second god. For in declaring that Christ is our Lord we learn how God *has completely given Himself to us, withholding nothing.* Words must be taken as they are, and nothing must mean nothing. God has given Himself in Jesus Christ. He is "a mirror of the Father's heart." This is the central affirmation of the divine Sonship of Christ. The Christian receives not something other than or less than God when he welcomes Christ.

Welcoming the Lordship of a defeated and dying Jew who lived little more than thirty years in a land which interests few of us is not the natural thing to do. Setting up the events out of which He is welcomed was not the natural thing for Christ to do. He became, He *has become*, my Lord, says the Christian. His becoming Lord was not automatic, either in the sense that He earned His status or that I earned my relation. He "became my Lord," says the Christian. This Lordship is asserted over the Christian, every Christian, at his baptism. But the Christian may not live up to or into his baptism; he may lose sight of the Lordship. Very often this failure or loss may be because he loses sight of the event by which Jesus became Lord. *Let this be the summary of this article, that the little word "Lord" simply means the same as "Redeemer."* The Christian must see what Jesus *paid and risked in order to win us.* The action by which He becomes Lord is asserted in the three cycles of the Christian year: Christmas, when *He became man . . . that He might become Lord;* Good Friday, when *He died in order to become my Lord;* Easter-Ascension, when *He assumed dominion at the right hand of the Father.*

With His coming, something new enters history and my story. God was in Christ, reconciling the world unto Himself. All power was "given" unto Christ; but He also won this power by His obedient death, "wherefore" God has highly exalted Him. God chose to win man back not by making a robot of him but by entering the conditions of humanity; He chose to win in the realm of the heart, which cannot be coerced. Jesus therefore came and followed the conditions of humanity to their inevitable conclusion: He died. He died alone, as all men must die. He redeemed and became Lord therefore *not with silver and gold but with His own precious blood.* We must remember that in the ancient world this reference to blood simply

(simply!) meant that a man died. So it was with Jesus. In the maze of injustices and the confusion of claims, His existence seemed to slip away, to be snuffed out, to come to no logical conclusion. But He was obedient, wherefore God exalted Him, and thus He became the Christian's Lord.

Since He came in weakness, humility, humanity; since He wooed instead of overpowered; since He won by love and not by dazzling authority, His lordship will be and must be asserted in the hidden disciplines of life. It may not show in any particular outward guise. The man of faith is not suddenly dyed green, he need not wear white clothes or a gold cross. He is not identified by adherence to laws and codes. Faith is born in the Christian, imagination is stirred, action is seen to conform with the masked Lordship of Christ.

But the Lordship of Christ also calls together those who would see it asserted. Christ comes to Christians in His congregation. He would be praised in the company of all who know Him to be Lord. Those who are baptized are baptized into His one death and resurrection; those who share His meal are participants in the one body; those who gather to hear His Word are drawn to each other, like iron filings crowding around a magnet. Jesus has won battles over the enemies of the community, whether they stand outside it or within it. This community may mean a Christian flock; it may mean a family. It is significant that the common table prayer for countless believers begins, "Come, Lord Jesus, be our Guest." He is to be the hidden organizing Center of personal life, congregational life, family life. He is to be recognized not only in the spiritual hours of obvious withdrawal but also in the common acts of the day's hours. "The loves we had were far too small," says a poet of modernity. Man loves, but loves what passes — what more is there to say? But when Christ is the organizing Center of all of life, when His Lordship is asserted and held with the full imagination, then that love is focused on what endures.

Here we have concentrated only on the assertion of Lordship without entering into a coherent discussion of the full Christian teaching concerning the meaning of Jesus Christ. A further word is necessary, however, to amplify a main theme of this meaning. The Lordship of Jesus Christ is asserted against the background of a cosmic drama, played out between good and evil, between good and evil in each man, between a benevolent God and malevolent enemies. What is more, it is seen against a background of conflict between justice and love (here language begins to break down) in the mind of God and in the world of men. This is the implication of the idea of Jesus' *risk*.

When God is described as saving man, this is done in terms of cost. Man is bought back, redeemed, from an alien realm. The Bible gives us many pictures of Jesus, but when it presents the Lordship-Redeemership picture, it intends to keep this concept of cost before men. It cost Jesus to become Lord over sin when He became man and suffered and died. Just what this means is difficult for Christians to assert. It is easier for them to point to the cross and with the earliest witnesses to assert, "He loved me and gave Himself for me." They can paint "Jesus saves" on the top of barns or on stones along the roadside. They find it harder to say who Jesus is and who man is and from what and for what He saves, and, hardest of all, why and how. Why the story of Bethlehem and the cross? Why this and not that other story? This raises an array of questions too complicated to be broached here. Here we must begin by saying that Jesus happened; He did not not-happen, and that makes all the difference. The Christian must puzzle out this one story, this one scandalous way God chose, and see God's working in it.

Obviously human language is a fragile instrument for dealing with the realities. Parable, comparison, analogy, metaphor, simile — one can run through all the pigeonholes and categories finding clues. The moment language takes hold of part of one category all the rest of all the others seem to disintegrate. Fully aware of this risk we might find it fruitful to grasp at just one of the countless illustrations of this plan in human action, one depiction of the tension between justice and love. It is third-handed; J. S. Whale quoting C. Ryder Smith quoting Peter Taylor Forsyth, who must have been quoting some historian's version of an ancient chronicle. Worn by so many hands and tongues, the story stands up well:

> Analogies furnished from human experience do not resolve that mystery [of Christology]; they serve only to state and leave it as such. [Take the] story of Schamyl, the chief of the fierce heroes of the Caucasus in their long struggle against the Russians. At one time some unknown traitor was giving away the secrets of Schamyl's little band, and he issued an order that the next person found communicating with the enemy in any way should be scourged. Presently there was an astounding solution to the mystery: the culprit was discovered, and it was Schamyl's mother. For two days he disappeared within his tent. Then he emerged, worn out with his misery and shame. He bade his men strip him and bind him to the stake, and to scourge him, instead of his mother, with the knout.

> That there is some analogy between this moving story of vicarious penalty and Calvary is obvious; but the limitation and ultimate irrelevance of such analogy is also obvious. For if there be any truth in the christological paradox that God was in Christ, we cannot hope to hold together in our minds "the objectivity of Christ's work towards God and its subjectivity in God." That would involve the absurdity that we could embrace the consciousness of God within our own consciousness.

> The story of Schamyl illustrates [only] the almost unendurable tension between conflicting loyalties on the human level. The story of Gethsemane and Calvary is, so to speak, on the two levels of the divine and the human, since as Son of God the Redeemer is at one with the Father, and as Son of Man he is at one with sinners whom He is not ashamed to call His brethren. The grace of our Lord Jesus Christ, which identified Him with the holy love of God, also identified Him with sinners completely and to the uttermost.

In this conquering identification Jesus becomes man's

Lord. He was buried that *He might make satisfaction for me and pay what I owed!* (Many people in recent years have run away from that term "satisfaction" because of some tortuous overtones; perhaps the story of Schamyl will help rescue it from misuse.) Jesus was born *that* He might become Lord; He died *that* He might make satisfaction; *all this in order to become my Lord.* In all three cycles the purposive aspect is clear: He did this so that His Lordship could be asserted. In that action is born the Christian ethic. "So that . . ." He would bring man back to God and conform man's life, now through the hidden discipline of forgiveness, to the life in God.

Each man of faith must ask himself, "Does it show?" Jesus is Lord, but that Lordship is today made visible through the sights and sounds of people. They become involved in the cosmic struggle, the never-ending drama between justice (because of evil) and love (because of God). Never-ending? That is not quite apt: the Christian's Second Article of Faith points toward a conclusion. This faith points toward a future when *He will completely divide and separate us from the wicked world, the devil, death, sin, etc.* God's purposes are not exhausted by the history of this world as it is now known. But this world is rendered terribly important because Christ's Lordship is asserted over it and in the middle of it. Christ identified with it. His work was not "out there" somewhere. He was born of a woman, under the Law; He was familiar with foxes, birds, winds, grain; He was dragged outside the city wall of the earthly city. In His resurrection He appears to men "in the breaking of the bread." His Lordship is seen among people, in the world, now.

The hidden discipline of the Christian life is born when the life of a person is hid with Christ in God. But it is classically expressed in the declaration, *I believe in the*

Holy Spirit, the holy Christian [catholic] church, the com-munion of saints, the forgiveness of sins, the resurrection of the body, and the life everlasting. The decisive con-nection is between the Holy Spirit and the holy Christian church; here the hidden life with Christ is sustained. It is this view that helps make sense of an apparent contra-diction in the disciplined life. At first glance this Third Article of faith seems to be purely a theological assertion, not a sociological one. That is, it seems to have to do only with the mind of God and His plan for the church; it has very little to do — one might think — with the way the church looks or with the arrangements of people in the church.

Can one not argue, however, that here, too, there is a consistent sociology of the church? Is it not true that not only the human institution, but also Christ's hidden flock is being made manifest here and there, now and again? Today more than ever in the past fifteen hundred years in the West some such view of the church presses itself upon our consciousness. It is a primitive view, but one that helps us cope with the realities of a new day. With it we can make sense of the church under the cross behind the curtains men drop. With it we can find morale to pick up the pieces in Christian cultures where the glue that held them together seems to be failing, the lubrication that helped them move seems to be spending itself.

What has happened? The external disciplines of a church in a Christian culture are disappearing. The legal authority of the church is not honored; it has lost its coercive power in the past few centuries. As a policing agency it is listened to less and less in a free society and in evangelical churches. Not only have the old codes and swords disappeared. The external disciplines of social cus-tom, manners, subtle pressures are being removed. More and more people crowd the world; their lives interact; they sit at home and are still bombarded by many kinds of signals and value systems. The church cannot be or cannot remain a nursery, a greenhouse, a sheltering and protecting agency. The church is thrown upon the inner disciplines of people who, having come to faith, want to conform their lives to the church's Head, Jesus Christ.

In such a day men will be tempted to misread the purpose of the church. Now when we are aware of setbacks on most fronts, there will be the temptation to exaggerate the successes. A man will climb into his tower and report on the condition of the church from where he stands. If he looks out on religious America in one of its periodic revivals, if he sees numbers of people attending and joining and building churches, he will suggest that all is well with the church. For him the basic strategy of the Christian life will be to flaunt churchly successes, to awe and overpower with statistical gains.

Such a view is bad theology and bad sociology. It is bad theology because it misorients the picture of the church's triumph in the middle of the world. Jesus told His disciples not to rejoice because the spirits were subject to them, because they awed and overpowered, but rather because their names were written in the book of life — they were hid with Christ in God. The view is bad sociology because it is simply untrue of the whole world for which Christ came; one cannot take the story of an island of prosperity and make it the whole world's tale. It will be believable on no score. Christians who seek morale to carry on their lives will have to learn from this Third Article of faith not to look to noise but to quietness for significance; not to listen for blunderbusses but for arrows; not to watch men blundering out into the world but men moving toward it with dovelike innocence, serpentine subtlety and finesse.

Is not this the whole pattern of God's movement toward man? Not in the thunder but in the still, small voice; not in Rome but in Bethlehem; not under Herod's gold crown but under Jesus' thorny one; not in the angelic legions but in the hidden flock; not with Caesar but with the Christian minorities; not concerned with empire but with church — such is God's movement. After he has learned to see Jesus

send men out as sheep among wolves, two by two, travel-
ing light — only then will man have the courage and faith
to turn over the church's life to its Lord. Then he can
transcend the false options of optimism and pessimism;
he can rejoice in what the divine life offers him in prosperity
or reverses. He will not pin the goodness of God to the
growth of the church but to its inner character.

Put it this way: if a flicker of faith in Jesus Christ is seen
in any person, take notice. If it is no more than the glim-
mer of a candle soon to be extinguished, if it seems on the
verge of being snuffed out — still, take notice. If it means
but one person participating in the new life, one man
in the pew, one woman involving herself in the hidden life
— this is more important than a new universe being born.
It IS a new universe being born: all things are new, this
is the creation. "God creates out of nothing — wonderful,
you say: yes, to be sure, but He does what is still more
wonderful: He makes saints out of sinners," (Kierkegaard).
This is creative work; this is the hand and breadth of
Spiritus Creator. This is what one affirms when he says,
I believe in the Holy Spirit. Such an affirmation is the
equipment for producing morale.

Now to see two people of faith doubles the miracle.
To see twelve was the immediate goal of Jesus. Jesus
"restricts nine tenths of His ministry to twelve Hebrews
because it is the only way to redeem all the Americans"
(Martin Thornton). I propose that this is the only sane
sociology of the church. The reason we cannot see this
fact readily is that after a millennium and a half of Chris-
tendom, it has become our habit to look only to the places
where power resides for the evidences of importance.

Now we are prepared to extend this view of the collective Christian life in several directions.

First, we affirm that God acts in creating the Christian
life in the church. Note the sequence: God the Holy Spirit
*first leads us into His holy community, placing us upon the
bosom of the church, where He preaches to us and brings
us to Christ.* If that statement is true, its consequences are

virtually immeasurable. Either its sequence is correct and Biblically faithful or it should be deleted from our consciousness. It asserts that God acts and that God acts as Holy Spirit in the church, where Christian faith is born. This affirmation runs counter to the whole idolatrous American picture of the church as a voluntary society of likeminded people who band together to suit only their own purposes. This sentence asserts that the church is both chronologically and logically, in time and in reason, antecedent to the individual Christian life and to the existence of particular congregations. We shall hear more of this assertion in our discussion of Baptism. Now let us see what it does to the current picture of organized religion.

A consequence of our modern world's separation of the realms of state and church has been a voluntaryism which throws the church on its own. Where numerous immigrations have poured together people of various Christian confessions into interacting proximity, the picture is complicated. It is further complicated by the fact that any entrepeneur can set up shop, can contribute to a cafeteria of religious impulses for sale in a free land. All this is so obvious we would not attempt to contradict it. But it has led to a mistaken measurement. It has permitted the original hidden significance of the church, the people of God, to be obscured. Even in the welter and confusion of denominationalism and the apparent or actual competition of Christian claims — even in this brokenness and chaos God acts and can act. The churches are born because the church exists. This is the judgment on all organizational self-seeking, all institutional self-aggrandizement. The Holy Spirit, instead, *has a unique community in the world. It is the mother that begets and bears every Christian through the Word of God. Where He does not cause the Word to be preached and does not awaken understanding in the heart, all is lost.*

Second, just as God acts in the church, so His Holy Spirit acts to unite. *This is the sum and substance of this phase: I believe that there is on earth a little holy flock or community of pure saints under one Head, Christ. It is called together by the Holy Spirit in one faith, mind, and understanding. It possesses a variety of gifts, yet is united in love without sect or schism. Of this community I also am a part and member, a participant and co-partner in all the blessings it possesses. I was brought to it by the Holy Spirit . . . .*

Again, this is a radical assertion of the hidden but real character of the church. There is in it no note of individualism on the pattern of the eighteenth- and nineteenth-century habit of deifying man alone. There is little accent on the struggle of will which we associate with a mass evangelism that directs itself efficiently to the individual: accept Jesus Christ as your personal Savior. The movement remains God's: "Console thyself, thou wouldst not seek Me if thou hadst not found Me" (Pascal). The evangelical witness makes clear that this seeking against a background of being found (the movement of the Third Article against the light of the Second) occurs with the church as a prior and fundamental fact.

Third, and the corollary of the two points we have considered, is this assertion: God acts to unite the centers of Christian lives. That He does so is seen in the other creedal aspects of the Third Article and in the consequent ordering of the church around the forgiveness of sins: *everything in the Christian church is so ordered that we may daily obtain full forgiveness through the Word and through signs appointed to comfort and revive our consciences* as long as we live. If everything is so ordered, then the various aspects of the church's life can be viewed from the center and not from the extensions, the tangents.

A real problem of Christian living based on individualistic, Robinson Crusoe views of the faith is this: if the church were initially man's creation, if it were a product of voluntary organizing, then the lives of people in it would be connected only tangentially, functionally, and not centrally. That is, two people worshiping in a pew next to each other, supporting a missionary together, peeling potatoes together, appear to be involved only at the edges of their existence where a temporary act unites them. But this view leads to all kinds of trouble. The imagination cannot be sustained to incorporate all Christians in one's memory and eye; one cannot know or care about the name of every missionary; one cannot care less about the success of a fish fry at a church two blocks away. Cannot one then dismiss the organized life of the church and insist on a spirituality of his own?

So Christians often go about seeing their lives bump each other's at the edges but not at the centers. We "affiliate" with "the church of our choice." This relaxed and loose way of talking about corporate life in Christ distorts Biblical reality. It is this distortion that furnishes the charter for competitive institutions; it is this that obscures the hidden meanings of the church's life. When the church is measured thus, it must build itself up through manifold subtle coercions, through false holds upon people. It must make laws or exert pressures or engender false claims. But if the Christian life is seen as a collective reality proceeding from one center, the forgiveness of sins, then nothing in the church or the churches is irrelevant or meaningless even if I cannot concern myself with the myriad details.

Lives connected at the center by the fact of their being hid with Christ in God: these are the products of the Holy Spirit in the church. The eye of faith sees this. One need not then be optimistic about a theology of the church to the point of romanticism nor pessimistic sociologically to the point of despair. The man of faith accepts what God gives in Jesus Christ and knows a peace that passes understanding, while keeping all his critical senses about him.

A further word is necessary about the phrase in the Third Article which follows witness to the Holy Spirit and the church. *I believe in . . . the forgiveness of sins. We believe that in this Christian church we have the forgive-*

*ness of sins, which is granted through the holy sacraments
and absolution as well as through all the comforting words
of the entire Gospel. Toward forgiveness is directed everything that is to be preached concerning the sacraments and,
in short, the entire Gospel and all the duties of Christianity.*

"Forgiveness of sins" is the generating power of the
hidden discipline! It does not mean that God slops over,
winks at, overlooks, does not care about, relaxes in the
face of, becomes casual about sin and the sinner. Such
an attitude on God's part would involve no death, no
dying; and only through death is new life born. Forgiveness of sins means that when man is exhausted in his moral
and theological quest, he turns his day back to God. He is
an unprofitable servant. He has done all that he could,
yet measured in the light of Jesus Christ is it nothing.
It represents a claim against God, a filling of the hands
with worthlessness so that God cannot fill them with worth.
At the point of man's exhaustion and extinction God steps
in by way of the cross of Jesus Christ and completes the
act. He annihilates, He smites, He stabs, He kills off sin
and the sinner. Then — and a whole universe is rearranged
for this "then" — He does a wonderful thing: He creates
something new. Not in the easy way this time, out of
nothing; this time it is the hard way, at the expense of
Himself (remember? He has completely *given Himself to
us*) in Jesus' death. Whenever the Christian imagination
is dimmed or the moral posture sags, the discipline that is
the corollary of forgiveness also disappears and grace is
cheapened.

Among those who wrestled with this liability in evangelical thought was Martin Luther, who is said to have
blurted out in his table talk: "Forgiveness of sins ought to
make thee rejoice; this is the very heart of Christianity and
yet it is a mighty dangerous thing to preach." A modern
poet recognized the risk; W. H. Auden recalls Luther this
way: " 'Justification by faith' he cried in dread, and men
were glad who never trembled in their useful lives."

62

The danger comes in the bookkeeping ideas that men associate with forgiveness as a transaction: I like to commit sins, God likes to forgive them; the world is admirably arranged. On this basis there is no room for growth in grace (indeed, no room for grace). There is no room for discipline, for coherence, for plot in life. So long as rejection of this self-defeating plotlessness is up to the individual alone, he will not be successful. Like the bushman who wants a new boomerang but does not know how to throw away the old one, he cannot get rid of his sagging, undisciplined picture of the Christian life.

The alternative is not the external discipline of Old Law or new custom. The alternative is the Spirit-given vision of the Christlike life, exposed, unsheltered in the middle of the world. Only then can goodness of Christian life proceed; *all who seek to merit holiness through their works rather than through the Gospel and the forgiveness of sin have expelled and separated themselves from the church.* But the forgiveness of sins, it is thus assumed, does produce holiness through discipline.

This view is far from every kind of perfectionism. The hidden discipline is more difficult, more demanding than the attempt to merit holiness. But he who practices this discipline is also visited readily by God, who re-creates newness. Its final victory comes only with the end-time. *Since holiness has begun and is growing daily, we await the time when our flesh will be put to death, will be buried with all its uncleanness and will come forth gloriously and arise to complete and perfect holiness in a new, eternal life.*

Until then there is the task of facing each day. The hidden discipline would be beyond our capacity if one had, today, to bear yesterday's faults and tomorrow's prospects. It is made to be spooned out a day at a time. The church is the fellowship of the daily unburdened. *All this, then, is the office and work of the Holy Spirit, to begin and daily to increase holiness on earth through these two means, the Christian church and the forgiveness of sins.* Daily: until the resurrection of the body is fulfilled, the life ever-lasting realized.

This, I know, is a fragile vision, a precarious mode of living. The alternatives are life under the Law or the subtle social pressures that have nothing to do with the Gospel. Life hidden with Christ in God through the Holy Spirit working the forgiveness of sins in the church: this is the only life the man of faith is to seek in order to live.

Here in the Creed you have the entire essence of God, His will and His work exquisitely depicted in very short but rich words. . . . We could never come to recognize the Father's favor and grace were it not for the Lord Christ, who is a mirror of the Father's heart . . . neither could we know anything of Christ, had it not been revealed by the Holy Spirit.

The Creed brings pure grace and makes us upright and pleasing to God. Through this knowledge we come to love and delight in all the commandments of God because we see that God gives Himself completely to us, with all His gifts and His power, to help us keep the Ten Commandments: the Father gives us all creation, Christ all His works, the Holy Spirit all His gifts.

To begin a discussion of prayer by placing it under the category of obedience instead of spontaneity may seem surprising. Prayer, a converse with God, sustains the life of hidden discipline from its first apprenticeship to its master craftsmanship. We are accustomed to thinking of prayer as the spontaneous outcry of the heart, the outraged or overflowing or burdened heart. It may become that. But Christian prayer begins in obedience and relies on promise, in spite of all other appearances. "In spite of" — these are the key words for understanding prayer to Christ's Father. *For whenever a good Christian prays, "Dear Father, Thy will be done," God replies from on high, "Yes, dear child, it shall indeed be done in spite of the devil and all the world."*

If all hangs on obedience and promise, then the daily repainted little pictures of prayer that we carry around with us need redoing. I have heard of a church whose walls and roof are shaped like a parabola — something like a croquet hoop, an upside-down "U." The architects explain that this shape imitates the arc a stone makes when thrown into the air and thus symbolizes prayer. Man throws his prayers to the heavens, and God drops His answer. It is hard to think of a worse, less accurate, less satisfying concept of Christian prayer. It is based on all those notions of man's striving to storm the heavens which, when snuffed out of our theology, bob up again in our piety. Had the architects wanted to express the human vision of prayer, they should have built a wall. Its straight line symbolizes how a man throws a prayer or a rock straight up into the heavens, and the force of its own gravity pulls it down and hits him on the head.

Invert the parabola and you have a different story. Just as God was in Christ reconciling the world unto Himself (the parabolic shape represents His initiative in drawing the world toward Him), so in prayer God condescends into the world of human asking and thanking and draws man back into His own world. This is the origin of the "Our Father" that leaps across the infinite chasms of silence which separate God from man. Here is where the great *"in spite of"* is born.

"In spite of" ourselves we pray to the Father. In our study of the First Commandment and in the First Article we saw that prayer so addressed was not natural. God the Father of Jesus Christ is not the product of man's fashioning. He has too many surprises, too many angularities, too many rough edges that just will not fit alongside man's household gods. If we pray without the initiative of this Father, we shall be praying to a false god, even if we pray within Christianity. It makes little difference whether we call Him First Cause, Supreme Being, Grand Architect, Great Force, or even, by an accidental scrabbling of syllables, Father: our prayers will be frustrated and hollow; they will fall like the rock thrown in a straight line or a parabolic arch.

Prayer thus evoked is at least a part of a latter day's unbelief. In a little church in Duesseldorf, Germany, I saw scratched in the stone a writing: "Ich kann nicht mehr beten" ("I cannot pray any longer"). It seems to many of us as if our fathers had it easier, as if belief communicated through prayer came more simply to them. Since we experience difficulty today, we tend to concentrate on the mechanism of praying, we worship man at prayer, we focus on our religiousness. This is but to erect one more idol and to shout at it until our throats are weary and our ears buzz.

The Christian keeps in mind the Father of Jesus Christ, who was mirrored in, yes, who gave Himself in the cross. This Father does not meet Dr. Freud's specifications of a father-image. He does not fulfill man's views of what fathers are like (remember our comment on the father of the Prodigal Son?). He is not just a big grandfatherly extension of earthly fathers, but is the absolutely greater prototype from which the picture of what is good in human fatherhood is drawn. Most of all, this Father is He and not it; He is addressed and addressable, *in spite of the devil and all the world.*

Again, in spite of what we see, God still commands prayer. *This is the first and most important point, that all our prayers must be based on obedience to God, regardless of our person, whether we be sinners or saints, worthy or unworthy.* This is a startling accent; without it, however, we deprive God of being God. *Nothing is so necessary as to call upon God incessantly and drum into His ears our prayer that He may give, preserve, and increase in us faith and obedience.* One prays because one obeys and one obeys because one prays — that is the circle. We have become dumb because we thought God was deaf. But we are dumb not because we are weary of shouting but because our vocal chords have atrophied. They have not been used until we pray because of a command. This is a misconception concerning prayer: that it is genuine only if it originates in spontaneous outcries. Prayer is work, hard work, spun out of obedience to command by a God who will not be denied.

We must also assert the parallel: in spite of what we hear, God still promises. *We should be all the more urged and encouraged to pray because God has promised that our prayer will surely be answered.* This, now, sounds like home ground for those who have heard the Gospel. The prayer is heard not because of the merit of the person who prays but because the Word of God is the source, fount, origin, and language of prayer, and God never denies His own Word. The man who first stumbles onto the language of prayer in obedience to a command soon learns that the forgiveness of sins opens the door to the more durable understanding of prayer in connection with promise. Prayer then is not just weather reporting, tuning oneself in on the infinite, meditating. It is asking, because not to ask is to doubt or deny God's promise and the very nature of

God. *A person who wants to pray must present a petition, naming and asking for something which he desires; otherwise it cannot be called a prayer.*

The idea of asking, of petition, is based on the remembered fact that in the "Our Father" it is Christ who prays. God hears because it is His Son who is speaking in every Christian prayer. In this sense, answering prayer is as natural to the Father as is breathing. That Christ identifies Himself with us and that we are thus identified with His prayer: this is the unnatural thing. This is the miracle, the unexpected. God speaks. God hears. We are not orphans, but His children.

Our Father. It is well for the beginner not to clutter his mind with endless formularies and learned treatises on prayer. He is sustained by two thoughts: If I believe, I will pray because (a) it is commanded; (b) it carries promises.

After this manner pray ye:

I

"Hallowed be Thy name."

What is it to pray that His name may become holy? Is it not already holy? Answer: Yes, in itself it is holy, but not in our use of it. The discipline of prayer begins in hiddenness and explodes into openness. It is hidden in that no one can force another to pray a genuine prayer. Social pressures may commit us to mumbling the Lord's Prayer in public worship because others around us are doing so. But to pray to a heavenly Father is a quiet, secret act, sustained in the privacy of Christian lives. Yet, if a man desires to remain comfortable and complacent, to pray that God's name shall be holy is what some people would call "inviting trouble." By praying he has interfered with God, or rather he has permitted God to interfere with him.

God's name becomes holy *when both our teaching and our lives are godly and Christian.*

In a sense, therefore, this first word of petition is the most extensive and inclusive of all. It is easiest to slide over en route to the more dramatic petitions about daily bread and deliverance from the evil one. But it involves what looks like interference with God and issues in God's interference with men.

Look first at God uninterfered with. To say "God" somehow implies that in the circle of His distance there is holiness beyond our understanding and our reach, holiness ineffable, ungraspable, abstract — and uninteresting. "Eternity bores us." But this prayer, accompanied by the faith which the Holy Spirit sustains in the community of the church, changes everything. God is now interfered with. God, the prayer asserts, has taken an interest in man and in Jesus Christ has involved Himself with the created world. This surprises us, that essence has to do with existence, that the eternal breaks into the middle of our world of subway transfers, broken bottles, caterpillars, and *Kyries.* For us to pray this prayer seems to bring about a change in God. More accurately, we could say it brings about a change in us that lets God's eternal character break through into our lives. We address ourselves to Him who listened even before we spoke. Then why pray? To make His name holy. Is it not already holy? *Yes, in itself it is holy, but not in our use of it.*

What becomes clear, then, is the change in the stance of man. Look at man uninterfered with, not caring about God, His name, His action. Man is uninterfered with, free to . . . Free? At this point he has not begun to be free.

> Life is not lost by dying! Life is lost
> Minute by minute, day by dragging day,
> In all the thousand small, uncaring ways.
> The smooth appeasing compromises of time. (Benét)

Man uninterfered with is man unchanged, playing out his appeasing compromises. But when this prayer is answered, God asserts His holiness in the middle of men and their world. Here is where the name of God plays its part. Man cheapens God until he speaks this word; then God acts. Man is interfered with. This means that our doctrine of God skews everything, reshuffles our conceptions. Then *our teaching and our life are godly and Christian.* The man who has prayed and meant this prayer is changed. Does he look it? The rabbi looked out the window when he heard the Messiah had come and said that he did not notice much difference. The philosopher said he could reject Christianity because the redeemed didn't look redeemed. Yet man is changed; the enjoyment of the divine name enters his life. Says Martin Buber, out of a Jewish (and thus in its first line Christianly unacceptable) orientation:

> If a man has fulfilled all the commandments, he is admitted to the Garden of Eden, even though he has not burned with fervor and has not experienced delight. But since he has felt no delight on earth, he feels none there either. Finally he even grumbles: 'And they make all that to-do about Paradise?' And hardly have the words left his lips, when he is thrown out.

Until man is interfered with by the holy name of God, he is free, free to yawn in the face of eternal life. But when he becomes good at names, good at the Name, he is wrapped up in its excitements. He can speak of God, but in proper terms, knowing (with Origen) that such speaking entails no small risk. That is what happens when this prayer is prayed.

"Thy kingdom come."

This second petition guards against the child of God's asking too little. It implies a large-enough prayer to a large-enough God for a large-enough life. Should a head of state or a rich banker or a gifted teacher offer you anything you

wanted, it would be ridiculous under ordinary circumstances to ask to have a shoe tied, a fly removed from the
soup, or a rhinestone dropped into the jewelry box. These
are things one can do or provide for oneself. They are
part of the overflow of a well-organized, healthy, serene
life. It is hard to tie the shoe if an arm is broken, to remove
the fly if one is nervous, to afford the rhinestone if one is
a miser. But these are insignificant matters alongside the
real issues of life.

Thy kingdom come — this is asking for everything all
at once. Again, the movement is the same as in the prayer
for hallowing God's name. As it was hallowed, so the
kingdom comes *of itself without our prayer, and yet we
pray that it may come to us.* To ask for the kingdom —
this is commanded. The kingdom is promised; Jesus teaches
the prayer to His circle of followers. As the head of state,
the banker, the teacher would be insulted by a small
request, a small expectation, so, too, the small prayer to
God is the mark of unbelief or unconcern and involves
the insult of the small expectation.

*Imagine a very rich and mighty emperor who bade a poor
beggar to ask for whatever he might desire and was prepared to give great and princely gifts, and the fool asked
only for a dish of beggar's broth. He would rightly be
considered a rogue and a scoundrel who had made a
mockery of his imperial majesty's command and was unworthy to come into his presence.* Is God to be bothered
with a child's fever, a malignancy, the problem of irregular
teeth or an irregular life, of a faithless wife or a foreboding
of economic recession? One cannot purge these immediate
concerns from the imagination; they loom large before the
petitioner. What is wrong in asking about them first is
that they are too small; they are the morsels, the beggar's
broth, whereas God would begin with the "whole business."

So one who has seen his life interfered with by seeing
God's name hallowed in it must be sure to begin with a
large-enough prayer: *Thy kingdom come.* By kingdom

something much more than the church is meant, though people sometimes casually confuse terminologies. The church presupposes the kingdom; the kingdom makes possible the church. The kingdom is not a place or a cultural era called "Christian"; it is the whole majestic and loving activity by which God saves man; it is personified in Jesus Christ. *What is the kingdom of God? . . . [It is] that God sent His Son, Christ, our Lord, into the world to redeem and deliver us . . . to bring us to Himself and rule us as a king of righteousness, life, and salvation.* This is a large-enough prayer; why does it bore us?

The answer is implied in the second concern: that it be prayer to a large-enough God. That is, we believe that God can concern Himself with small things like "spiritual" matters but are disturbed at His impotence in the affairs of daily living. Your God Is Too Small, shrieked a book title some years ago. Another book (by Stephen Bayne) spoke about an "Optional God": "We do not readily deny God's existence; but we look at the possibility of God as at best a helpful supplement to the real dynamics of life. It makes no fundamental difference whether He exists or not." The problem of unbelief is squarely faced in this petition. To pray for the kingdom of God is to ask that one's own small view of God be shattered, that God be permitted to break through into all of life, that one's priorities of living be rearranged. It remembers Christ's words: "Seek ye first the kingdom of God and His righteousness," but then does not forget that "all these things shall be added unto you."

The fruit of a large-enough prayer to a large-enough God will be a large-enough life; *therefore we must strengthen ourselves against unbelief and let the kingdom of God be the first thing for which we pray.* Such a prayer gives a new outlook upon life in the kingdom as well as to life in the church. In fact, it gives a new goal to this life; it means to build up the church but to build it not through laws and power plays but through the gentle equipment of the Gospel of peace. "To build the church is not to build up a solid institution which is wholly at home in the world and uses the methods of the world. It is rather to organize a band of pilgrims who are on the way to a new and better country and who must therefore not adapt themselves to their temporary surroundings" (W. A. Visser 't Hooft). Such pilgrims are carefree, for they are pre-adapting themselves to their permanent surroundings; in the realized kingdom, they belong. The pilgrims are sons and daughters.

"Thy will be done on earth as it is in heaven."

Next time you pray this prayer, do not say, for once, "Thy WILL be done," but "THY will be done." This change of emphasis makes all the difference. It also introduces an element of surprise into the most misused of all petitions. How is this prayer usually regarded popularly? Listen for a while and you will hear people pray it usually in a spirit of resignation or acquiescence. They use it when they are at the end of their rope or when they throw in the towel. Everyday piety translates this prayer thus: "God, I wanted things my way, but they are not turning out that way. So I shall turn them over to You, for Your competitive will has more power than mine and will probably have its way anyhow. So teach me not to grumble too much about how things are going against me." In the background one hears the sweet organ tones and almost smells the overabundance of flowers in the funeral parlor: *Thy will be done.* Our war is over. I give up.

Not at all! Here just about the opposite is implied if with Jesus we accent the three great "Thys" of His own prayer. Instead of resignation, here is militancy; instead of acquiescence, here is a declaration of war. Here the life of inner discipline erupts into external action, asking only that its acts be found consistent with God's will. In one sentence: to pray this third prayer is to invite trouble. This prayer is to be shouted, not whimpered; to be announced, not whined; to be chanted, not tentatively breathed.

When the Lord's Prayer is prayed, the Christian invites trouble. *If we try to hold fast these treasures* [God's glory and our salvation in the first two petitions], *we must suffer an astonishing amount of attacks and assaults from all who venture to hinder and thwart the fulfillment of the first two petitions.* The enemies of the good have nothing to fear from goodfellows, milquetoasts, and assorted well-meaning individuals. They will quake in the presence of those in whose lives God is active, hallowing His name, breaking in with His kingdom. The Christian lives in a besieged city, leads a besieged life. Then he compounds the foolishness by inviting opposition as he calls God to be ranged with him in human history.

Enemies of the good will not easily give ground against this hidden aid. Superficial prudence would therefore suggest that the Christian would do well to overlook this prayer, not to pray it, let it alone. He will then have ventured nothing and will have gained the same amount. The Christian becomes a big-game hunter, however, and he needs big weapons. If Christ ranges Himself with His Father's children, then these people are themselves standing in Christ's place. Injustice once before attacked Christ, and can do so again. There is a war on. Shallow cease-fires dare never deceive. Band-aids are not good medicine for cancer. Earmuffs may dull the sound of guns but not cause them to be silenced. The Christian seeks the peace of victory. *"Thy will be done on earth as it is in heaven."* Since "in heaven" God's will no longer meets opposition, this prayer asks that the will of God, which will be done of itself, shall be done among us, that we participate in the activity of bringing its opposition to an end. This is why the enemy is alerted to recognize it as a fighting word.

So far so good. What the one who prays the prayer neglects to notice until the agony begins is that the battle is not swirling around him but within him. When this agony comes, he is lost in mystery. What defect of vision, what limit of hearing prevents his facing and conquering it? Why does he compound the agony by inviting God to conquer him? So he seeks evasions. He can stop praying. He can take the escapist way out. He can rail against the heavens and end in despair. He can turn cynical. Thomas Hardy's epitaph for one of his characters is in this spirit: "The President of the Immortals finished his sport with Tess." The Bible does not claim to give all the answers for the human predicament; but we can be very clear that among the answers it gives that is not one. Men are not puppies tumbling at the feet of an Oriental potentate. They are creatures destined for a hidden life in God, who identified Himself with them at their worst, who was "made sin for them, [He] who knew no sin."

The petition also implies a new strategy for the warfare. It asks that one's life be conformed to God's will consistently and persistently. Often people give up in a marital trouble, complaining that they cannot adjust and God cannot hear. They blame God for the sudden disruption. But they have habitually refrained from this prayer, and have thus prevented God from winning. Now their ears are stopped. When war is imminent, pacifists are often scorned because they have no plan, no pattern. But the war became imminent because long beforehand all parties involved failed to conform their lives to the will of God. This prayer asks that God's will break in to break all that hinders man's participation in the divine life.

When it is answered, the Christian can count on a majority of two. *One or two Christians, armed with this single petition, shall be our bulwark, against which the others shall dash themselves to pieces.* This prayer breaks the will of the most powerful enemies of God. THY will, not "Thy WILL," be done. Someone's will is going to be done. It may as well be God's.

IV

"Give us this day our daily bread."

Here we consider the poor breadbasket — the needs of our body and our life on earth. . . . This petition includes everything that belongs to our entire life in this world; only for its sake do we need daily bread. In these words the earthy character, the world-oriented concern of the Christian life, is made clear; the hidden discipline is made manifest. For with these words the believer stands among all the other men and women of his time, needing and having, lacking and being supplied. But he stands among them as one who acknowledges his Father and Forgiver as Source of all these earthly goods. Therefore, as he prays, all the concerns of the Christian faith are included. Foremost among them is the command: Have no anxiety about anything; take no thought for the morrow; your heavenly Father knows your need. Freedom from these anxieties liberates him to have honest concerns because of this prayer. We shall note several of them.

First is a concern for the bread itself, the bread for which he prays. Bread is the actual and the symbolic minimum of the world's diet; it represents all other gifts of the body. "Bread for the World" as a slogan summons up people's best impulses for giving all types of material goods to others. One does not have to list pepper and persimmons, overalls and underwear, shelter and protection. "Bread" stands for all these. This symbolism is what adds to the integral beauty of a loaf of bread. One need not undertake an analysis of the molecular structure of its elements, need not be an artist and paint a still life including bread (as many have done). He will someday sit at a white-clothed table and perceive the clarity of a glass of water and the directness of a piece of bread and — if he is hungry — he will understand the earth's potential. The man who prays "Give us this day our daily bread" is not asking "Give me the minimum" or "How can I gain the maximum?" He is being asked to enjoy the bread that is set before him and the life that is given him.

But if bread is good in itself, if it actually fills bodily need, it also implicates man in a second concern: for all that bread implies. Now it means not only everything in the Sears, Roebuck catalog. It means *also peace and concord in our daily business and in associations of every description with the people among whom we live and move.* We can hear these words in their Biblical setting; we can think what they meant in 16th-century rural or village society; but we should be able to see even more in a modern, technical, and interrelated world how necessary peace and concord are for the daily needs of life. In the violent political situation, in the international uncertainty, we have seen what unrest can do to the supply of "bread" for daily life. "The nerve of life is missing if small things are missing." Small things will be missing if the big things are out of line.

It would therefore be fitting if the coat of arms of every upright prince were emblazoned with a loaf of bread instead of a lion or a wreath of rue, or if a loaf of bread were stamped on coins, to remind both princes and subjects that through the office of the princes we enjoy protection and peace and that without them we could not have the steady blessing of daily bread. The condition of the world has not changed much since late-medieval times; revolution and famine, warfare and depression are all related to man's daily quest for bread, for peace and concord.

Third, the man who prays this prayer has a concern for the God who gives bread. He is witnessing to all who stand in hearing range of this prayer. Bread here is a sign of the existence of God (not to all, but to the man who lives the hidden life).

Rabbi Levi Yitzhak once summoned the townspeople to meet in the town square to hear an important announcement. The merchant resented having to leave his business. The housewife protested against leaving her chores. However, obedient to their rabbi, the townspeople gathered together to hear the announcement their teacher was to make.

When all were present, Rabbi Levi Yitzhak said: "I wish to announce that there is a God in the world."

That was all he said, but the people understood. They had been acting as if God did not exist. While they observed ritual and recited the correct order of prayers, their actions did not comply with the commandments of God.°

The prayer is said in the light of the fact that God gives bread, like the rain and the sunshine, to good and bad alike; to those who say "Our Father" and to those who make themselves into lords. But the believer as he prays this prayer is saying (and then inviting observation of his conduct): "I wish to announce that there is a God in the world."

This is another way of saying that the man who prays is giving thanks not only for the bread but for the hand that supplies it, the divine arm that reaches out to him. He gives thanks unto the Lord and "forgets not all His benefits," particularly the gift of Christ and His benefits. He draws nearer at times when only the hand and not the gift is seen. Often, when after 29 good years of marriage, the 30th, bad year comes; or after 14 years of peace, a 15th year of hostility comes; or after 12 years of work a year of unemployment comes — in that year the hand of God is recognized as it had not been when it was full. But the man who is then drawn near to God is less likely to forget the hand that gives.

Fourth, this prayer implies concern for the man who receives the gift unthinkingly. It is prayed by the hidden flock for the larger group that never cares to examine the source. It is a return from earth of a song of praise in behalf of those who do not care by those who have enjoyed

° William B. Silverman, *Rabbinic Stories for Christian Ministers and Teachers*. Abingdon, 1958, p. 127.

the sun, the rain, the bread, the peace and concord. It is thus a prayer prayed in the face of the Enemy, *whose whole purpose and desire it is to take away or to interfere with all we have received from God.*

Again, praying this prayer indicates a concern for the other, the brother who is also implied in the *"Our* Father." This concern is seen supremely at the Eucharist, where Christ comes into the middle of the world in a meal and with bread. This prayer is prayed as a blessing over the bread and wine at the Lord's Table, and with good reason. He who has shared with others the hidden discipline of the forgiven life, who has thanked God for Christ and all His benefits, returns to the bread of the earth thankful that with Christ God freely gives him "all things." This is why wise men in the church today urge that, in the face of Acquisitive Man, Organization Man, Market-Oriented Man, we develop "Eucharistic Man" as the free man. Eucharistic Man is sent from the Table with only one assurance: not that there will be bread but rather that he will not have need, because his Father knows his need. He will be free of anxiety, of self-pity, so long as he is sustained by the Eucharist and lives on its sustenance.

Sixth, it should go without saying that this prayer shows concern for the man who is in need, and thus it enlarges the scope of petition for earthly things into intercession. It is loving the neighbor on one's knees.

The corollary to this is a concern for the man who shares. If man honors God as the Source of bread and wine, peace and concord, then he becomes a steward, a good custodian of his portion of a generation's resource. The man who returns the first and large part of these gifts for the Lord's service is master, not servant of his possessions. That he is master is certifiable in the lives of all good Christian stewards. It is theologically made clear in that in the sharing of the bread with the hungry all is done "to the least of Christ's brethren."

Eighth, it is the concern of this prayer that gives life to all the others; namely, concern for the Christ who teaches.

His meals shared with crowds and disciples on the green grass of Galilee and again in the hidden life at Emmaus and in the Upper Room are all incorporated in this prayer that He taught. After all, "they knew Him in the breaking of the bread"! His meals, His miracles, His appearance, His stories — how often they involve the bread for which He taught us to pray. In the kingdom of the new age He would again eat a meal with His disciples. He would eat it with the fulfilled community which now in fragmentation prays for daily bread and gives thanks for the heavenly bread. This petition is the greatest, briefest parable we possess from the lips of Jesus.

V

"And forgive us our debts, as we forgive our debtors."

This petition sustains the hidden discipline. *Whatever can be effected by Baptism and the Lord's Supper, which are appointed as outward signs, this sign also can effect to strengthen and gladden our conscience.* It is a prayer attached to promise more than to threat, and can be rephrased by a man in private: *Dear Father, I come to Thee praying for forgiveness, not because I can make satisfaction or merit anything by my works, but because Thou hast given the promise and hast set Thy seal to it, making it as certain as an absolution pronounced by Thyself.* In this light, the prayer looks different than it did before.

One may look at something 999 times and be perfectly safe, it has been said; "but if you look at it the thousandth time, you are in danger of seeing it." Nine hundred and ninety-nine times this prayer has been prayed; we have been tempted to use it as a means to hook God to our achievements, to put a price tag on our act of forgiving others. Now we see that it is prayed by the forgiven who hear, *Not on account of your forgiving* does God forgive. It sounds as if Jesus were making the one exception here, making God's action secondary to and dependent upon our achievements. But if we begin by seeing the forgiveness of sins as the shaping act of the new creation, the new life, matters are seen differently.

If God takes the initiative, why should we pray to be forgiven *"as we forgive* our debtors"? Only for one reason: unless we forgive others we cannot experience the new life; we will not know what forgiveness is, will have no criterion for measuring the gift of God. After a man has seen this, his act of forgiving others is seen in a new earnestness, however much it grows out of his new freedom.

Forgiveness by God and by men is so serious a matter because of the seriousness of the way in which forgiveness disturbs the old creation. People who gripe over coffee about their neighbors and make common-sense observations about the state of things in general are often most severe and judgmental. But they will resent hearing about sin in the churches, and for one reason: precisely because there sin must be taken with absolute seriousness; because there an absolutely different kind of measurement is used, a true plumb line is dropped into the congregation of believers. There the ego is finally assaulted. Outside the church, observations concerning the conduct of others can always leave refuges, islands, havens for pride. I determined what was evil and then measured others. "Forgive *us* our debts" properly locates the measurement with the forgiver. It is then less easy to point at an Adolf Eichmann and an Adolf Hitler; I must look at 1535 Wildway Circle and see my part. Does the universe grind to a halt as God observes my shortcomings? In a way, yes: it is my shortcoming that prevents the new creation from breaking in with fullness. The creation groans and sighs, awaiting the redemption. That redemption, that new creation breaks in when a man is forgiven.

Then, only then, because he understands and in order to understand the new creation (this is all one act), he forgives others. When he prays this petition, he is not solving all the world's problems. He is, however, doing

something extremely important. He is saying, The process
of avenging must be reversed somewhere; it is being reversed here! The process has been reversed by God, but
now it is being reversed among men. People who have
been genteel but grudging about their grudges, petty about
their pettiness, keeping score on spouses, neighbors, nations,
suddenly see the cost God pays to effect newness. They
range themselves with Him, and at cost to their own pride,
their own measurement, they forgive. Man "lowers his
plumes before God." God acts; then man acts toward his
brother.

Forgiving the brother is never the precondition of God's
forgiveness or the attention-getter. It is the new way of
life of the one who has renounced his rights to play God,
to be judge, to establish the stands of his own integrity.
The roadblocks and barriers are removed. When a man forgives, it is not that the number of his brother's sins against
him are reduced from, say, 764 to 763; rather he sees the
neighbor in a new setting, from the angle of vision of Jesus
Christ at the point of the shout "It is finished!"

Then there is no point in keeping quiet score so that in
the next marital battle the partner's minor vices can be
dredged up, resurrected for public display and private hurt.
There is no point in trying to gain the advantage. There is
no point in contriving the secret hurt of another. Man is
free from the necessity of engaging in such practices and
may become more nearly free from the temptation to do so.

Why? Because he prays with Jesus Christ, the only one
who never has had to say, "Forgive me my debts." Christ
was tempted as we are, "yet without sin." He carried His
temptations to a cross and to victory. His victory and His
righteousness are the gift of God to man. The forgiven life
is visible in Baptism and in the Lord's Supper. The dancer
Pavlova was asked to interpret in words one of her dances.
She replied, "My God, do you think I would have danced it
if I could have said it?" As with her act, as with sacred
acts, so the common acts of life reveal the hiddenness of
the forgiving life. That life is not all enjoyment; one can

no longer indulge in the luxury of nursing grudges. He must say farewell to them. He has rejoined the family of Jesus Christ, a family that has the criterion for hearing the word of forgiveness and the capacity for experiencing the release that forgiveness brings. Its members are forgiven, as they now — characteristically and customarily — forgive others.

VI

"And lead us not into temptation."

We have said that the Christian who prays the Lord's Prayer is inviting trouble. The electronic organ tones we associate with Malotte's "Lord's Prayer" throw us off guard almost to the point of blaspheming the intention of the prayer. It is not a saccharine, soothing, spiritual slumber-party inducement; it is a battle cry, a shout for the end time, a rallying banner for the hidden flock of Jesus Christ as it becomes open to *"Our* Father's" response. Nowhere is this made more clear than in this sixth petition. It does not concern itself too greatly with the minor vices of life, except in that succumbing to them is part of a great betrayal. Rather this prayer must be prayed because if Jesus Christ is truly formed in a man, it is Jesus Christ in him that is tempted anew. The enemies of the good life are armed only against Jesus Christ, and they will assault the man who lives his life in Christ.

Temptation may be seen positively as a trial, negatively as a seduction. But most of all it has the positive-negative polarity in mind: it appeals to man's faith or nonfaith. Petty vices are not the main distraction. The greatest saints are known to have noticed pretty girls; reasonably ethical prophets have been known to take a nip. But both saints and prophets were in the orbit of real temptation in those or other acts because the Christ in them was being assaulted by His one great enemy.

What could they do? They were not asked to be catacombed, cloistered, conventicled: Jesus had sent them out into the world. They were not asked to be less than human, to drain themselves of emotions, passions, loves, concerns for life. They were asked to be the most intense of people. They were never to become robots, manipulated by God away from human concerns; they were not bottled up in baptismal water and prematurely shipped off to heaven. They were to move as Christ had done, in the middle of the world, but "with an otherness that was unmistakable" (G. Bornkamm). The best help they got was from shouting this battle cry, "And lead us not into temptation."

What is clear, then, is that temptation is not removed but accented for the Christian. To be human is to be tempted; to be a Christian is to have this human susceptibleness heightened. *Temptation is of three kinds: of the flesh, the world, and the devil. . . . Youths, for example, are tempted chiefly by the flesh; older people are tempted by the world. Others, who are concerned with spiritual matters (that is, strong Christians) are tempted by the devil.* It is the third concern (as we shall see from Part VII) that predominates when the Lord's Prayer asks for victory. Sometimes in the spiritual life there is an apparently superhuman concentration of antireligious energy: "Has God said?" More often the spiritual life is quietly eroded, hedged about, rendered comatose, killed. Where God works among men, there is also temptation.

A good translation of these words could be, "Snatch us not away in the hour of temptation." For the semifinal, penultimate forms of temptation are related to the final, the ultimate forms. This is the prayer for the end time: "My God, my God, why hast Thou forsaken me?" God is not to abandon His hidden flock and its members in the evil hours of their existence. Family, finance, success, self-dignity, keeping schedules: all these can be penultimate distractions. But in the end they are always part of a big distraction: the death of the spiritual life, hell made visible. Against this God is asked to wage war.

The man who prays this prayer is often the one who has seen temptation conquered, only to face worse temptations. He is telling himself and advising others, "Do not become overconfident." But he also has an answer: temptation is conquered through identification with the Father. The petition turns out to be very practical: this is, exactly, how things work out. For that reason the prayer is described as a refuge: *your only help or comfort is to take refuge in the Lord's Prayer and to appeal to God from your heart.* The final victory is assured: God did not abandon Jesus Christ. The one who prays this prayer is identified with Christ in the middle of the world. He still has enemies, an enemy: *but prayer can resist him and drive him back.*

VII

The last petition is closely related to the sixth and may have been phrased as part of it. *But deliver us from evil. Amen.* The New English Bible New Testament translates these phrases,

> And do not bring us to the test,
> But save us from the evil one.

This translation was criticized by some sentimental admirers of the King James version and by defenders of the traditional versions that are badly sung at countless weddings. The critics would have done well to ask, first, which translation more accurately presents the sense of the original so far as it can be determined; and, second, which version can do most for the Christian life, which has the more dramatic impact.

We cannot settle these questions here; for our purposes we must let it suffice to say that this newer translation better parallels the interpretation which is before us. Not: Our Father, we would like a life of ease, don't tempt us;

don't let evil things happen to us. Instead: Snatch us from the test, the great temptation; save us from the evil one! This is again a battle cry of the man in Christ. *In the Greek the petition reads, "Deliver or keep us from the Evil One, or the Wicked One." It is he who obstructs everything that we pray for: God's name or glory, God's kingdom and will, our daily bread, a good and cheerful conscience, etc.* Evil is personalized, made more vivid, more dramatic, more realistic. This is how we confront it in daily life. So, too, in prayer.

Even the evil things that come upon the body are seen in this personal contact as the result of the working of God's enemy. *Therefore there is nothing for us to do on earth but to pray constantly against this archenemy.* "Deliver us from evil" is the last petition and should not be prayed first (in the style of foxhole religion). It is not merely the prayer that asks God that nothing bad or even very exciting may ever happen to me. It is the summation: after the name is hallowed, the kingdom comes, the will is done, then it is seen that the Evil One has intensified his attacks. The fact that the devil is no longer pictured as a gnome or a little man in a red union suit does not reduce the drama of the personal character of great evil. The devil may have gone underground in the third-person pronoun instead of the second, "he" instead of "you." He may have really burrowed in under the neuter "it" instead of the personal "he." His application blanks could be filled out, we are told, with this description: "Outstanding characteristics or markings?" "None." But the experience remains unchanged, whether in the concentration camps or in the suburbs.

Prayed at the end of the Lord's Prayer, this petition comes at the end of the struggle. It shows that the evil one has failed to take Jesus into account. An athletic coach may hate a player and therefore put him to more use where the action is thickest. In the process he develops a more durable, a better player. Jesus, the Man of God's own choosing, enters the world; despised there, He is put at its battle lines, where opposing forces clash. He is the Durable One. His gift is that those who follow Him are also sustained against the evil one. If prayed last, this prayer helps us to understand the nature of prayer. It is not a magic spell that helps us escape evil or bail us out when we are tired of using our own resources. It is the foreign language, long strange but now become our own again as we are disciplined to lead the hidden, forgiven life, conversant with Christ. That is why the Lord's Prayer is prayed in the church. There it is rescued from any aura of the superstition it takes on when it is embroidered on pillows, stamped into pennies, engraved on amulets worn around the neck. In the church it is rather carried above the head as the mark of discipleship. It is the Lord's prayer, prayed by His followers. Out of the depths they cry. They are snatched from the evil one. They have faults and fears that they have not even become aware of, but they *ask in faith,* expecting to receive.

"I am for going on, and venturing my eternal state with Christ, whether I have comfort here or no. . . . I will leap off the ladder even blindfold into eternity, sink or swim, come heaven, come hell: Lord Jesus, if Thou wilt catch me, do; if not, I will venture for Thy name." The Lord's Prayer is not "going to sleep music"; it is martial, for it calls to action. But the man who prays it knows its hidden reality. He does not look protected. But he is.

I

The hidden discipline issues in public acts and is sustained and nurtured by public acts. Central among these public acts are Baptism, confession, and the Lord's Supper. Baptism is the beginning of the Christian life and must be dealt with first. *What is Baptism? It is not simply common water, but water comprehended in God's Word and commandment and sanctified by them. It is nothing else than a divine water, not that the water in itself is nobler than other water but that God's Word and commandment are added to it.* Accent on Baptism does not mean that we are now at the stage where loose ends, peripheral teachings of the church, must be fitted into a scheme or a plan. Baptism is, in miniature, a complete picture and a decisive act of birth, of discipleship, of death, of resurrection. It *is* the Christian life.

This understanding of Baptism is difficult to come by in a culture that sees it as a cute little cultural act at which a name is given, a white dress worn, and the grandparents are asked in for champagne breakfast. Baptism in its essence meant dying; for Christians in many ages it was the visible public break with the world, the break inviting trouble from the world. It was not something that happened to me long ago, when I was young. It involved survival for the Christian person and the church. One could define the Christian life as the attempt to live up to what is implied in God's act in Baptism.

Water and the Word. One must do justice to both. The Reformers of the church for the most part scurried past the meaning of water in order to come to the power of the Word. Their emphasis is understandable. In many ways they were involved in opposite kinds of battles than the church of our time has. They were fighting magic, superstition, a universe too readily peopled by demons and angels who were subject to man's manipulation through certain acts. Accent on the power of water in the sacrament could have fed this confusion. We today face a desacralized universe, a matter-of-fact naturalism which will not allow God to revisit and work in His own creation. The Reformers fought the false materialization of sacred acts; we fight the false spiritualization of sacred acts. God works through external things, they kept insisting; we shall have to give double weight to this emphasis in order to sustain it at all.

Why is water important? Because it is clean, clear, sparkling, healing, nourishing? No, because it is the creation of God over which His Spirit brooded; because through it His people passed on the way to deliverance; because into it Jesus stepped to fulfill all righteousness; because Jesus left commands connecting it with the agency of God. *"How can a handful of water help the soul?"* *Of course, my friend! Who does not know that water is water, if such a separation is proper? But how dare you tamper thus with God's ordinance and tear from it the precious jeweled clasp with which God has fastened and enclosed it and from which He does not wish His ordinance to be separated?* God involves Himself with material things and sends the Christian to live his life among them. No attempt is made to give a magic power to water for its own sake; no, *the water is not different from that which the maid cooks with and could indeed be called a bathkeeper's baptism.* But even water that a maid cooks with has a tremendous actual part in our lives (indeed an essential one), and it has an equally great symbolic power.

Here again many people are afraid of the Freudians, who have pointed out the connection between water and baptismal bowls and rites of passage in the physical and psychic life, and Christian Baptism in the religious; or of the sociologists who have seen Baptism as a familial act of the church, satisfying needs for symbolic integration. Why Christians should be embarrassed in the face of these

views is difficult to discern. Of course, many of them veer
off into contrived and eccentric interpretations. But basically they point to a valid issue: Baptism and the Christian faith concern themselves with our physical and psychic
and familial makeup; they take the commonness of our
bodies' meaning and transform them to a different potential. This understanding of the fact that God reaches into
His order, our world, and shapes out of water a new act
of creative power means that He would hallow this life.
It was the water, the basic combination of elements that
was used for the sacrament; it was not honey, not milk, not
pomegranate juice. In the new creation even more than
in the old the Holy Spirit broods over the waters, and something new comes of it.

In old and new creations, the Word was decisive. "And
God said . . ." "By the word of the Lord were the heavens
made. . . ." "He upholds all things by the word of His
power. . . ." All is done *by virtue of the Word, which is
a heavenly, holy Word which no one can sufficiently extol,
for it contains and conveys all the fullness of God.* The
creative Word of God sustains the Christian life; it annihilates sin and sinner, meaninglessness and despair; it creates something new — order out of chaos, life out of death,
resurrection out of crucifixion. The water has no independent life; it is the Word working in it that effects order and
life and resurrection. No wonder that for Paul "Baptism"
can take on almost all the connotations which "discipleship" had in the Gospels; here is the break with the old
self for the sake of freedom to be immersed in the middle
of the world and through it in a new creation. In Christo-
pher Fry's play *A Sleep of Prisoners,* a number of British
soldiers are billeted in a German church. They muse about
their lives and the meaning of their location. One asks
what they are all doing there; another answers, "You were
born here." That is Baptism in its nature and essence. *To
be baptized in God's name is to be baptized not by men
but by God Himself. Although it is performed by men's
hands, it is nevertheless truly God's own act.*

II

Secondly, we are concerned with the purposes and benefits of Baptism. Here we can be direct: *to put it most simply, the power, effect, benefit, fruit, and purpose of Baptism is to save.* A young minister preaching at a mental hospital was interrupted by a patient who had the insight to hear sermons: "All those words are very pretty, Reverend, but just what did you have in mind?" A discussion of Baptism boils down to having one thing in mind: Baptism exists to save. Though it is related to the First Article of the Christian faith in that it uses a creative element, and to the Third Article in that it is the door to holiness, the Reformers concentrated all their attention on having one thing in mind: Baptism is to save.

So simple, is it not? And yet, the moment we hear that word it is complicated. Who saves whom from what, for what, and how? How are we rescued from the slogans and formulas that declare, Jesus saves! and immediately ask, Are you saved? What do they mean for our lives? What is more boring than to hear the same old thing: salvation? Does not this word answer a question that is not being asked? If I am bored with hearing words of salvation in this life, will it be any more exciting to know of an eternity of the same? Somehow, with the wisdom of the Scriptured ages, the word still holds the answers and the excitements for a new kind of age's questions. "To save" (*'yasha*) comes from a Hebrew root word that relates to giving spaciousness, to removing confinements. "He brought me forth also into a large place," said the ancient man who feared the narrows and ravines where his enemy's arrows and surprise attacks could defeat him. He wanted openness, the plain. Baptism addresses itself to a more inclusive rescue from the narrows, the constriction, into the large place of Christian freedom. *To be saved, we know, is nothing else than to be delivered from sin, death, and the devil and to enter*

91

into the kingdom of Christ and live with Him forever. Christians today are and should be edgy about seeing their faith dismissed as a salvation cult, an escape valve out of involvements in the world of men. Yet they see that being saved, being brought into a large place in the middle of the world, frees them.

Rescue is a real need in daily life. The housewife climbs the four walls after being imprisoned hours on end with the children. The executive needs escape from the mold into which he is forced. The laborer wearies of the eight-hour routine. The farmer measures out life in a meaningless sequence of days. At three o'clock in the morning each lies awake and sees the straitness of his own experience, the infinitesimal spatial significance of it, the brevity of the moment of time granted. He is anxious; he has come into the narrows. In such a time, many escape from freedom to new authoritarianisms. Others are dazzled and blinded by apparent freedom and are lost without signposts. Still others surrender to the apparent finality:

> "Alas," said the mouse, "the world is growing smaller every day. At the beginning it was so big that I was afraid, I kept running and running, and I was glad when at last I saw walls far away to the right and left, but these walls have narrowed so quickly that I am in the last chamber already, and there in the corner stands the trap that I must run into. "You only need to change your direction," said the cat, and ate it up.*

The Christian answer to such despair, erraticism, escapism, centers in Christ; this answer is connected to the cross by Baptism. There "salvation," the "large place," the health, wholeness, spaciousness of Christian freedom is a benefit of God's action. In Baptism an ancient people delivered through the Red Sea lives again, as they make their way to the Promised Land. Baptism is such a gracious water of life. Its visibility shows that God concerns Himself with life in the middle of this world; its visi-

* Franz Kafka, *The Great Wall of China.* New York: Schocken, p. 209.

bility is also its offense. Some reject it because it relates to sense-experience. Yet Baptism *must be external so that it can be perceived and grasped by the senses and thus brought into the heart, just as the entire Gospel is an external, oral proclamation. No matter where he [God] speaks — indeed, no matter for what purpose or by what means he speaks — there faith must look and to it faith must hold. We have here the words, "He who believes and is baptized will be saved."* Christ "became what we are that He might make us what He Himself is" (Irenaeus). Once God revisited this creation and showed us what man is; He made visible in the middle of the world a Savior. Baptism extends Christ's benefits to all. Here is "room to breathe."

In Baptism, therefore, every Christian has enough to study and to practice all his life. For Baptism is intimately connected with faith. When the legal props and social pressures are removed, man lives not by Law but by Baptism — by repentance and freedom. *No greater jewel, therefore, can adorn our body and soul than Baptism, for through it we obtain perfect holiness and salvation, which no other kind of life and no work on earth can acquire.*

The life of hidden discipline begins routinely as a man makes the sign of the cross on arising, praying, dedicating the day to God. This salutary act is a mark of repentance; his old self has died and a new day for a new man begins. It is a mark of dedication; it quietly turns over this body from its own pursuits to God's working. Most of all, it is a mark of identification. Once the cross was signed over this body with the water and the word. A name was given. A person was dying, being buried with Christ so that he might live with Him. The cross left no visible mark; its arcane, secret quality calls him to the act of faith afresh each day. Baptism conferred and signified the gifts. It said something and it did something. Here was the great break between man and flesh, man and Law, man and sin.

But the day thus marked, turned, dedicated, identified calls a man to something new. Baptism is not the mark of a marketplace grace that licenses him to do as he pleases; it is the mark of a cross that calls him to conform his will to Christ's. Each act of the day looks different then; none is insignificant. The architect who fussed over details replied, "God is in the details." So with the hidden details of the day disciplined by Baptism-repentance. *We must draw strength and comfort from it . . . we must retort, "But I am baptized! And if I am baptized, I have the promise that I shall be saved and have eternal life, both in soul and body."* One of the great impoverishments of the Christian life today is the failure of the church to teach people thus to use their Baptism. The testimony of Christian experience speaks clearly of its liberating influence. Baptism provides a place on which to stand to view the world, to receive an organized grasp of its complex, to reorganize an opposition to its chaos.

Baptism is, finally, baptism into Christ's body, into a redemptive society. It was Christ in the church who both presented and received the infant in faith in Baptism, who called the adult to death and new life. *We bring the child with the purpose and hope that he may believe, and we pray to God to grant him faith. But we do not baptize him on that account, but solely on the command of God.* Should a man deny the benefit? *Gold remains no less gold if a harlot wears it* in sin and shame. The power of Baptism resides solely in the Word as it reaches and is heard in the believing community: *"I come here in my faith, and in the faith of others . . . [but] on this I build, that it is thy Word and command."* The faith of others here aids me. In Baptism I am crucified with Christ, nevertheless I live. I am not alone; a quiet inner discipline holds together those who are truly disciples in the hidden flock of Jesus Christ.

CONFESSION

+

I

There is a false evangelicalism that has heard the Gospel and made of it a nothing; it has lapsed into chaos and lost its discipline and purpose. If Baptism (and, we shall see, the Lord's Supper) offers complete, exhilarating, inclusive comfort, one can let one's conscience sag. *Everyone knows this now. Unfortunately, men have learned it only too well; they do whatever they please and take advantage of their freedom.* What ties them to the hearing of the Gospel, the activation of their Baptism, the renewal of their meal with their Lord, is an act called Confession. It does not have independent status and can be discussed under either Baptism or Lord's Supper. Thus:

Here you see that Baptism, both by its power and by its signification, comprehends also the third sacrament, formerly called Penance. Penance transformed by Baptism-Lord's Supper becomes confession. The restoration of confession to the evangelical churches — as both a public and a private act — will be the test of the seriousness of the hidden discipline. With surprising suddenness we have discovered — almost too late — that the neglect of confession has meant a relapse in the modern world of Christians into two false ways: legalism and relaxation. Under the quiet roofs, along the broad, tree-lined avenues of our villages, in the glass and steel of our apartments, on our farms, live people who use gentility to cover up terror. They use politeness to cover up loneliness; apathy to cover up despair; escape to cover up the vacuum that will not let us be alone with ourselves. In the face of this condition, people of other professions who deal with persons ask the evangelical churches why they have given up their greatest disciplinary and therapeutic treasure, confession of sins and absolution.

On the one hand, with or without confession there can be too much accent on the guilt and terror of life. There

95

can be a pessimistic, narcissistic fascination with disregarding the seriousness of sin. Such a life is short on purpose and responsibility. The Reformers insisted on confession as a voluntary act, not a legal demand. In their passion for seeing the whole being of each man reoriented to God in Christ they were uninterested in the arithmetic of "how many" sins. The sons and daughters of the Reformation allow confession to disappear because God disappears for them. Where God reappears, "if I believe," then the seriousness of His demand is recognized again. Where do men take their problems? "My doctor says . . . My psychiatrist advises . . . My counselor suggests . . ." But God seldom is permitted to intervene in the coziness of these arrangements.

What does confession look like in the pattern of hidden discipline? It is always interpersonal: I confess to my pastor or in private to God or to my brother or neighbor. The Christian confesses to his pastor because he knows it is never advisable to confess to a superior, and his pastor is a minister, a servant of his spiritual life. A superior will be a judge on his own terms, imposing his own standards; a man who confesses to a superior thus delivers himself over to an enemy. A minister must "come from below," drawing sanction from the gift out of the past made present by the Holy Spirit: forgive as men confess. A minister symbolizes a personal relation reopened to the humanity against which one has sinned. Because he is ordained to hear confession, he is equipped by role, training, and seal to listen and to bear a confidence. He did not earn the right to hear: he is a representative person.

The Christian confesses to God in any case, in private or in public. But God always works through the external, through Baptism, the Lord's Supper, the Word which absolves.

In the third possibility, the Christian confesses to his neighbor in special circumstances. All wrongdoings against another are confessed to the other. But wrongdoings against man and against self may be confessed to any other confidant, a concerned Christian who is a joint debtor to the grace of God.

More important than the "to whom" is the "how and what" of confession. Confession always occurs in the light of the Law of God, which annihilates any pretensions. Similarly, it always occurs in the presence of Jesus Christ, whose image is a judgment upon me. Certain techniques for self-examination are prescribed. They can be viewed as the steps by which one determines his hunger for the Lord's Supper. Suppose I feel no need to confess. *I know no better advice than to suggest that they put their hands to their bosom and ask whether they are made of flesh and blood.* Unfortunately this technique does not work too well in a conscienceless world where the reminders of mortality and the attachment to the temporal bewilder more than they stir to action. This worked for the sin-sick soul; it does not work for modern man in his health, prosperity, comfort, and well-being. But it is he who most of all needs to confess.

A second technique is open, though it is seldom tried with any sense of seriousness. *If you cannot feel the need, therefore, at least believe the Scriptures. They will not lie to you, and they know your flesh better than you yourself do.* They are an infallible, unerring guide for diagnosing the spiritual condition of man. They quicken and activate themselves through repeated consultation; they cannot work in the man who permanently removes himself from hearing range.

For the man who will not read the Scriptures there is a third means: the reading of periodicals, newspapers, signs of the times. *Again, look about you, and see whether you are also in the world. If you do not know, ask your neighbors about it.* (As a matter of fact, almost any neighbor will be running around with a little list of faults, grievous faults he has observed in his neighbor; he will be most willing to oblige.)

The fourth means, seldom real to people today unless the other three work in them, is the reminder *you will*

surely have the devil about you. He who was challenged
by the end of the Lord's Prayer and routed in Baptism
takes one more try — each day — recovers lost ground. He
has proved his own nonexistence and thus has complicated
— and made doubly necessary — the act of confession.

The Christian has a great stake in the development of
the imaginative literature and the arts of his time; which
is to say, in better diagnoses of the human situation. When
the imagination atrophies, confession subsides. As a corollary to belief, the imagination is quickened, and man's sense
of presence before a holy God in responsibility is awakened.
Without this quickening and awakening, people carry a dif-
fuse sense of guilt, experience a nagging instead of terror.

The important points to recall in the act of confessing
are two. First, the quality of the confession does not imply
an interest in enumerating. Such arithmetic only distracts
from the gravity of a whole life turned away from divine
purpose. Second, guilt is made visible in relation to the
form of Jesus Christ with which one has been identified
in Baptism.

What would recovery of confession do for the world?
Would it be but one more self-preoccupying, man-in-the-
mirror, inverted concern of a church? We cannot speak
for the whole world, but in our society some 60 percent
of the people claim to want to stand in the arena where
the Word of God can get at them. Not all that goes wrong
in slum and suburb, Washington and the state capital, fac-
tory and office, is the fault of the 40 percent who are not
in hearing range. The 60 percent are asked, in confession,
to become what they are: baptized. *Therefore, when I urge
you to go to confession, I am simply urging you to be
a Christian.* This may mean man on his knees in public
worship; it may mean pastoral counseling; it may mean
a quiet Saturday afternoon's chat turned suddenly serious
and grave; it may mean a reestablished formal private act;
it may mean a word spoken to the neighbor. *Confession
would be rightly taught, and such a desire and love for it
would be aroused that people would come running.*

II

So long as it relates only to Law, confession is self-indulgence, narcissism, fascination with psychology. The life of hidden discipline is made free the moment it experiences the parallel or opposite act called absolution. "I absolve you" means that now God has created a new thing, a forgiven person. Because absolution is born in Baptism and related to the Lord's Supper, it is seen as a churchly act. This does not mean that God works only through ecclesiastical channels; anyone can speak the word of forgiveness. It means, however, that what is everyone's task is no one's task; hence Jesus gives to His church the power, the command, the promise to absolve. There is no magic here. There is rather a profound and radical separation from the old life. Absolution is, in the evangelical tradition, a borderline sacrament — a sort of sacrament of sound waves, an acoustical matter in which the word "I forgive" is not only an announcement but an act.

G. K. Chesterton said he joined the church "to get rid of my sins." Absolution transforms that affirmation from what could easily become a selfish one into a liberating and yet responsible corollary: absolution rids G. K. C. not only of but for something: He is free for service in a world that needs it. When a man is absolved, his broken relation with God is restored. He hears the word from a human, and thus is restored by a person and as a person. The word is heard here, in the middle of the whole messy human involvement, not "out there" in some heaven of heavens. By giving this word to the church, Jesus is not saying, "Forgive and forget" but rather, "Let Christ live in you." This counsel has a psychological validity. It removes one from the constant crossfire of human measurements. The psychiatrist who tells the person who says, "I feel inferior," "You *are* inferior," is clearing the air with an impressive act of honesty. But this was not the word the man needed from another man. "You are forgiven" — that is the word. This is a more expensive word than the one spoken after a 15-dollar half hour on a couch. It wrenches man from what he held onto in the past, up-roots him from the security of his nursery.

God uses special times and places to heighten and in-tensify experiences and acts which are always at least potentially present. So at the beginning of each day, or at the end of a week, or on the day of the Lord's resurrec-tion, the arena is cleared and the word "You are absolved" is heard. Some people are offended to hear a human say, "I forgive you in the name of God." They should be; their indignation shows an alertness to the sacredness and drama of an act which, viewed slightly off-angle, would be blas-phemous. Who can forgive sins but God only? (It was a tribute to the Reformers' times that men cared that much about the holiness of the act!) People should still be of-fended to hear the word; only thus will the precariousness of God's venture in giving men the power to forgive be sustained. Only then will the reminder of the world-enwrapped Gospel be clear. Once more, it is here in the middle of things that the word is heard. Indeed, only God can forgive. But He has sunk His hearing in the deaf-ness of mortals (Buber). Here is the test of the forgiven life: After the knee joints of the confessing one have knicked back into erectness for pace, for walk — what will his life look like? He will still belong to time and space, to a world of catalogs and barometers, family dinners and lonely nights. Here he needs the word, and God gives a church, gives in it men and women to speak and act in His name. *Thus by divine ordinance Christ Himself has entrusted absolution to His Christian church and com-manded us to absolve one another from sins. So if there is a heart that feels its sin and desires consolation, it has here a sure refuge when it hears in God's Word that through a man God looses and absolves him from his*

CONFESSION ✛

sins. . . . The word of absolution . . . is what you should concentrate on, magnifying and cherishing it. Need confession then be coerced?

As a hart longs for flowing streams, so longs my soul for Thee, O God.

I

The Word Made Flesh described life in the kingdom of a new age as a banquet at which the bread and wine would be eaten and drunk in fellowship with Him. This depiction of the future is the prototype for a meal shared on earth, as the climactic celebration of the Word among men. It is called the Lord's Supper. Its relation to the hidden discipline of Christian living is obvious once its nature is understood: *The Lord's Supper is given as a daily food and sustenance so that our faith may refresh and strengthen itself and not weaken in the struggle* but grow continually stronger. For the new life should be one *that continually develops and progresses. The Supper is a treasure, which is daily administered and distributed among Christians.* No external discipline brings the Christian to this meal: *no one should under any circumstances be coerced or compelled.* But those who absent themselves *are not to be considered Christians.*

Serious words, these, about an act which many churches tack on four or six times a year after the sermon so that an ordinance is kept. The drama of the words is hard to appreciate in the middle of a ritual in which immaculately dressed women promenade forward to receive an almost plastic-looking wafer in the name of a dying God; and well-groomed men reach their week's hygienic peak as a drop of wine touches their lips from an antiseptic individual glasslet. Hard to picture, is it not, the mystery of an age when participation in this meal marked a man for death and life. But the same activity of God is celebrated and present in both ancient and modern meals because it is the real coming of His Word that sustained and sustains each participant. Our discussion, as with Baptism, proceeds from the essence of the meal to its benefit to its use.

Essentially, the Sacrament of the Altar *is the true body and blood of the Lord Christ in and under the bread and*

*wine which we Christians are commanded by Christ's word
to eat and drink. The sacrament is bread and wine, but
not mere bread or wine such as is served at the table. It
is bread and wine comprehended in God's Word and connected with it.* It is the voice of God accompanying the
hand of God to satisfy the restlessness of man and quicken
him to new action. It is the presence of the Word in a hut
or a chapel or a cathedral where the "This is My body,"
"This is My blood" is spoken. It is the anticipation of the
heavenly feast among men and women whose lives are all
too obviously earthbound. It is the answer to the question,
"Who am I?" in an act that says, "You are found in Christ.
Your life is hid with Christ in God." It is a means of God's
grace being channeled into the life of men.

And it places upon man a crisis of belief. If people could
arrange for Christ's presence in Galilee or Chicago, Naza-
reth or Tokyo, all would gather — it is said. But the one
who has heard the word of the Lord's Supper knows,
"Christ is here!" Yet He comes again as the despised and
rejected, the neglected, unknown, and unloved. Some observe His coming too infrequently to witness to His presence. Others absent themselves when His resurrection is
celebrated each week. Do they believe? Is it only their
imagination and not belief? How shall we answer this
when we have Jesus' clear record according to the Gospel
that He was leaving only to return with a more, not a less;
with a more real presence and a greater joy. When He
came and they ate in His presence in the resurrection, they
were changed, ready to die for Him. They did.

Failing to recognize Him now seems then to be an aspect
of unbelief more than apathy. Men locate themselves instead in the sacramental mimicry of the cocktail party,
where cordiality and acceptance seem to prevail. They
take their problems to the counselor. They assert the authority of their physician. This is all well and good; but
the life of hidden discipline is not nourished as Christ
stands alone, His real absence attested to all the world
by His nominal flock.

The solution is found in the awareness in faith of the presence of God in the form of Christ's activity. He who "reflects the glory of God and bears the very stamp of His nature, upholding the universe by his word of power," now comes with ordinary bread and wine in an extraordinary presence. This is no place to undertake a doctrinal exposition of what is implied in the Lord's Supper. In each of these chapters one can hope at best to anchor a theme in a word. Here the connection is with the Word of the cross of Christ. The Lord's Supper indicates participation in the body of that death; it is a separation from those who reject Him; it is the celebration of the life found in Him; it is the unmerited invitation. The Lamb of God, whose praises are sung just before the meal in the historic liturgies, is again the dedicated, solemn Victim in the middle of the world's injustices. The death of His self meant life for all who, receiving Him, are to know the death of their selves.

If this act is understood, everyone is changed. The queen stands here — if only here — on the same level with the commoner, the millionaire with the miner, the bored housewife with the overexcited collegian, the pimply adolescent with the man grayed by age. (Regrettable, is it not, that sociology and snobbery sometimes militate against this transsectional view of its reception!) Here is an action shaped with a word. The bread of the old creation and the hopes of the old covenant are taken over into the new creation and the new covenant in Christ's blood. In it the Gospel is recapitulated. The lady in Scotland who approached the table, changed her mind, indicated to the whispering, inquiring clergyman that she could not be at this table for she was a sinner, had the bread thrust at her: Here, take it, it is for sinners! Precisely. It is the banquet of the unacceptables, the highwaymen and hedgemen who are now asked to bear in their bodies the wounds of Christ and to let the glories of God shine through in their hidden lives along highways and hedges.

II

Now we come to its power and benefit, the purpose for which the sacrament was really instituted. . . . This is plainly evident from the words just quoted, *"This is My body and blood, given and poured out FOR YOU for the forgiveness of sins."* As Baptism exists to save, the Supper exists to forgive, and these acts and gifts are one. *"How can bread and wine forgive sins or strengthen faith?" This treasure is conveyed and communicated to us in no other way than through the words "given and poured out for you."*

Here you have both truths, that it is Christ's body and blood and that these are yours as your treasure and gift. . . . Now, the whole Gospel and the article of the Creed "I believe in the holy Christian church, the forgiveness of sins" are embodied in this sacrament and offered to us through the Word. "Forgiveness" and "for you" — these are the hinges on which understanding of the Lord's Supper hangs. God's act and man's person are involved in this participation in the body and blood of Christ.

Through this meal the Christian life takes on a new perspective. "I am writing a great sermon on sympathy and do not have time for individuals," is the blasphemous word of the Organization Church. The belief in a purely spiritual encounter is refuted by the visibility of this material action. God acts. He acts in Christ. Christ is present. He is present in the sacrament. If a man believes that, his whole life is a disciplined and joyous acceptance of what God chooses to give in Jesus Christ.

Any student of the Bible, any historian of Christian tradition, knows that it is an oversimplification to interpret the Lord's Supper solely from the viewpoint of forgiveness of sins unless forgiveness of sins can come to encompass the whole definition of the Christian life. The Biblical overlay of meanings includes many other ideas, but they are now corollaries of the forgiveness. There is the mystery of the act in the plan of ages. There is presence. There is communion. Obviously, Eucharist or thanksgiving plays its part; even sacrifice cannot be wholly neglected — there is Biblical witness to each of these celebrations of the fruits of the earth wedded to the Word.

Each of these, however, breaks through around the act of forgiving and being forgiven. The Lord's Supper is the pledge, the sign, the gift. Here the ego is shattered and the man in Christ formed. The problem for the man preparing for this meal is not that he is too self-centered (though that is part of the problem), but rather that he has not seen himself on a big-enough scale of divine purpose and potential.

The old sermons of New England were designed to lift men above their chores and to point them to a quest for clarity, for a North Star. So the Lord's Supper should remove the chaos and diffusion of daily life and place men where God can reach them with His call that they die and live with Christ. For you. For forgiveness. Many ideas and one idea are captured here. The words of the Pax Domini of the liturgies which precede Communion indicate well its gift: "The peace of the Lord be with you alway." And the congregation responds, "Amen." It will be this way. This is the act of faith that makes it ours. This is the comforting and liberating element of participation.

Who should come to the Lord's Supper? Who is the "you" of the "for you" in the Lord's Supper? Here is our last opportunity for witnessing to the character of this life which hangs on faith and the Word. For the last time, as in Biblical and Reformation times, the "you" is not for the man who merits but the man who hungers, not for the man with full hands but with outstretched hands. Man faces a troubled world. He is not really free for facing it. He has difficulty discerning how God's purposes are not exhausted by the meaningless present. He is in his body and cannot escape it. He hears, "For you," and takes, eats, drinks, walks away to new, responsible life.

He now possesses a treasure that must be put to use. *The treasure is opened and placed at everyone's door, yes, upon everyone's table, but it is also your responsibility to take it and confidently believe that it is just as the words tell you. . . . These words . . . are not preached to wood or stone but to you and me; otherwise Christ might just as well have kept quiet and not instituted a sacrament. Ponder, then, and include yourself personally in the "you" so that He may not speak to you in vain.*

Here is the evangelist calling for new (daily) decision; here is a sawdust trail that leads to a stairway to an upper room; here is the anxious bench where the *"Come to Me . . . and I will refresh you"* is heard. Why do Christians have difficulty accepting this invitation? A man cannot come if his hand and heart are full. A prisoner with his hands full of hack-saw blades is not open to accepting a key that will give him freedom; a child who is carrying two large quartz rocks will not notice the diamond; a man parading his securities is unready for the newness. That is where confession (see the previous chapter) comes into relation to this sacrament.

Do this! There is a command; the One who won man's freedom now offers the command with its promise. The disciple follows to please, the baptized man to live out the parable of death and life, the weary one for comfort. Man has the liberty to reject the gift, but not the liberty then to be free.

This is the gift which, like all other open enactments of the Word, sustains pilgrims who have their eye on the city which has foundations, whose builder and maker is God.

107

The hidden discipline is the forgiven life that lives neither under the annihilating Law of God nor in the realm where His grace is accepted in slovenly fashion. The discipline is hidden because no Law from the past and no social pressure from the present environment regulate it. The hiddenness is disciplined because life needs a plot, an organizing center, and because only such a life is really free of the chaos of a time. This life is addressed by the Ten Commandments, its judge; it is expressed in the Creed, its formula; it issues in the Lord's Prayer, its battle hymn. Between the Baptism which gives it birth and the Lord's Supper that points to its fulfillment, is the confession and absolution which daily frees man for responsible life. The Christian life is effective to the degree that in faith Jesus Christ is permitted to live in it, in the form of a servant. It asks, "If I believe, what does my life look like?" It is sustained by daily recall of the mighty acts of God who in many and various ways spoke of old to our fathers by the prophets, but who in these last days has spoken to us by a Son.

> Therefore let us go forth to Him outside the camp, bearing abuse for Him. For here we have no lasting city, but we seek the city which is to come. Through Him then let us continually offer up a sacrifice of praise to God, that is, the fruit of lips that acknowledge His name. Do not neglect to do good and to share what you have, for such sacrifices are pleasing to God. . . . Now may the God of peace, who brought again from the dead our Lord Jesus, the great Shepherd of the sheep, by the blood of the eternal covenant, equip you with everything good, that you may do His will, working in you that which is pleasing in His sight, through Jesus Christ; to whom be glory forever and ever. Amen. (Hebrews 13:13-16, 20, 21 RSV)

I. N. J.